Penobscot, Maine

near Dennysville, Maine

Back Roads of New England

BY EARL THOLLANDER

Clarkson N. Potter, Inc./Publisher   NEW YORK
DISTRIBUTED BY CROWN PUBLISHERS, INC.

Published by Clarkson N. Potter, Inc., One Park Avenue, New York, New York 10016 and simultaneously in Canada by General Publishing Company Limited

Manufactured in the United States of America

Library of Congress Cataloging in Publication Data
Thollander, Earl.
  Back roads of New England.
  1. New England—Description and travel—
1981-   —Guide-books. 2. Automobiles—
Road guides—New England. I. Title.
F2.3.T47   1982   917.4'0443   82-486
ISBN: 0-517-547120   AACR2
ISBN: 0-517-545950 (pbk.)

10 9 8 7 6 5 4 3 2 1

First Updated Edition

to my wife,
janet

Contents

Hazen's Bird House
Westford, Connecticut

Martin houses at
Meadowbrook Farm,
Canterbury, Connecticut

Greene Herb Gardens,
Greene, Rhode Island

Preface

This book is an on-the-spot pictorial record of the villages and places I have seen and enjoyed while traveling the back roads of New England. It would be a monumental task to catalog all the delightful back roads in New England. My book is a selection from these roads, a somewhat circular tour beginning in Rhode Island and ending in Maine.

I have not really attempted to outline a tour of New England but rather to inspire you toward your own route selections and back roads adventures. I would suggest that when you wish to go from town to town, and since back roads maps are scarce, ask locally about roads other than normal highway routes. (Get it down on paper, too, so you can't get lost!) That way you may discover a different, more "earthy" New England.

My pace for travel on the back roads ranged from five to thirty miles per hour. This brought me into closer contact with the countryside, for at these speeds I could easily stop to view a scene or talk with someone. At the outset of my travels I stopped to ask a fisherman at a back roads bridge the name of the small tree that was blooming profusely in the area. He said, "That must be the shadbush." He then added with a friendly smile, "Would you like some fish?" I accepted and later enjoyed fresh trout for lunch. The beauty of the shadbush in bloom and the friendliness of a lone fisherman got my travels on the back roads of New England off to a memorable beginning.

Shadbush

author's note

The six sections of this book all begin with a state map showing the back road areas and associated towns. Official state maps, available free from Travel Services, Chambers of Commerce, Tourist Bureaus, Automobile Clubs, and other sources will direct you to these areas. My local maps should then guide you successfully along the back roads. If you get lost, hopefully you will find yourself on an even more interesting route.

Rather than writing detailed driving directions on how to get onto each back road I have put as much information as possible into the local maps. Distances, village names, road names, when designated (not many were posted in Vermont, New Hampshire, and Maine), nearby highways, and other helpful hints are on the maps themselves. The thicker map line is the back road trip recommended, the arrow is in the direction I traveled (which certainly could be reversed if you were so located) and the North Pole, as it is traditionally indicated, is toward the top of the page. Maps are not to scale due to the diversity in length of many of the roads; however mileage notations have been made where they seem necessary. Useful to me in discovering the back roads of New England were maps furnished by the highway department of each state. The scale used was one inch to the mile which meant that for Massachusetts alone I had to deal with an unwieldy ninety nine maps, each measuring 13½ x 18 inches!

Map Legend		
▬▬▬▬	my backroads route
———	other roads
··········	more primitive roads
▲ 3m ▲	distances between points in miles
– – – – –	boundaries of lakes, ponds and rivers

Rhode Island

    Of the six New England states
Rhode Island is the only one small enough
to be able to show back roads with sufficient
clarity on their official state highway map.
This is a great boon for the inquisitive traveler.
The Rhode Island coast is quite interesting and
popular, however my travels carried me also to the
rural villages, farms, and forests of the state.
    It may be surprising to strangers to
Rhode Island that this tiny state has such
beauty along its interior back roads.

True Forget-me-not

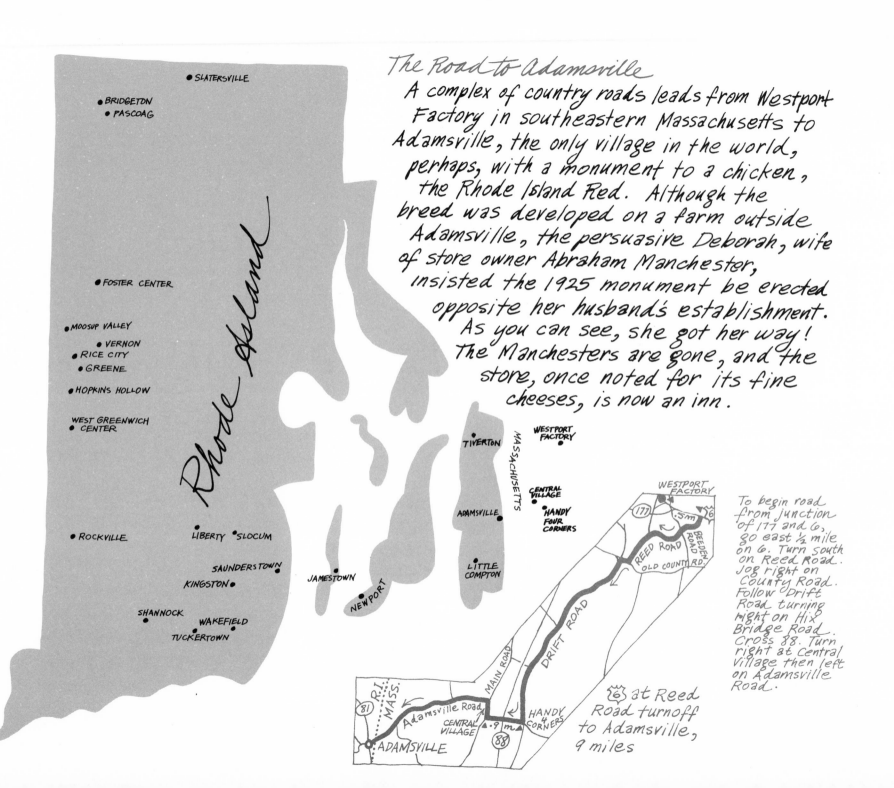

The Road to Adamsville

A complex of country roads leads from Westport Factory in southeastern Massachusetts to Adamsville, the only village in the world, perhaps, with a monument to a chicken, the Rhode Island Red. Although the breed was developed on a farm outside Adamsville, the persuasive Deborah, wife of store owner Abraham Manchester, insisted the 1925 monument be erected opposite her husband's establishment. As you can see, she got her way! The Manchesters are gone, and the store, once noted for its fine cheeses, is now an inn.

Rhode Island

SLATERSVILLE
BRIDGETON
PASCOAG
FOSTER CENTER
MOOSUP VALLEY
VERNON
RICE CITY
GREENE
HOPKINS HOLLOW
WEST GREENWICH CENTER
ROCKVILLE
LIBERTY • SLOCUM
SAUNDERSTOWN
KINGSTON
SHANNOCK
WAKEFIELD
TUCKERTOWN
JAMESTOWN
NEWPORT
TIVERTON
MASSACHUSETTS
WESTPORT FACTORY
CENTRAL VILLAGE
HANDY FOUR CORNERS
ADAMSVILLE
LITTLE COMPTON

To begin road from junction of 177 and 6, go east ½ mile on 6. Turn south on Reed Road. Jog right on County Road. Follow Drift Road turning right on Hix Bridge Road. Cross 88. Turn right at Central Village then left on Adamsville Road.

6 at Reed Road turnoff to Adamsville, 9 miles

WESTPORT FACTORY
177
.5m
6
REED ROAD
OLD COUNTY RD.
BEEDEN ROAD
DRIFT ROAD
MAIN ROAD
HANDY 4 CORNERS
CENTRAL VILLAGE
.9 m
88
R.I. MASS.
81
Adamsville Road
ADAMSVILLE

Adamsville, Rhode Island

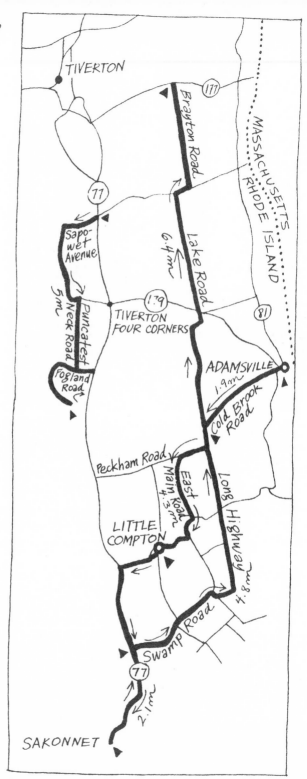

TIVERTON

177

Brayton Road

MASSACHUSETTS
RHODE ISLAND

77

Sapo-
wet
Avenue

Lake Road

6.4 m

5 m

Puncatest Neck Road

1.79

TIVERTON
FOUR CORNERS

81

Fogland
Road

ADAMSVILLE
1.9 m

Cold Brook Road

Peckham Road

East Main Road
4.3 m

Long Highway

4.8 m

LITTLE
COMPTON

Swamp Road

77

2.1 m

SAKONNET

From Adamsville pass Westport Harbor Road
on the left to take the road to Little Compton.
later, traveling Swamp Road, pass Long Pasture
Road, turn right just before the big 90° turn,
then almost immediately left to reach
Long Highway.   Note: Fogland Road becomes
Pond Bridge Road when it reaches 77.
Additional Note: Sapowet is also Seapowet
Avenue locally. My official Rhode Island map
read Sapowet.

Roads to Little Compton and Tiverton.
   Impressive are the long walls of stone
along these roads, carefully fitted together
without mortar. They look as if they will
stand forever. On Fogland Road I drew
a wall. The setting sun was on my back,
warming me against the crisp sea breeze.

Stone wall, Fogland Road

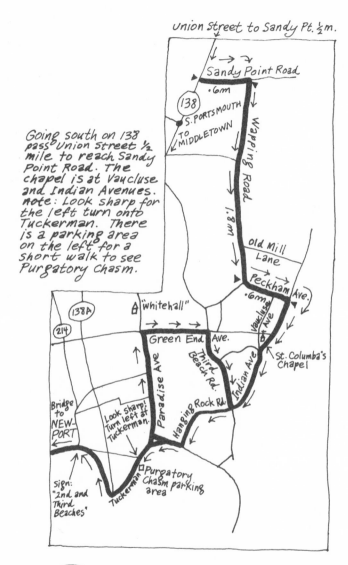

Union Street to Sandy Pt. ½m.

Sandy Point Road

.6m

138

S. PORTSMOUTH

TO MIDDLETOWN

Wapping Road

1.8m

Old Mill Lane

Peckham Ave.

.6m

Vaucluse Ave.

Going south on 138 pass Union Street ½ mile to reach Sandy Point Road. The chapel is at Vaucluse and Indian Avenues. note: Look sharp for the left turn onto Tuckerman. There is a parking area on the left for a short walk to see Purgatory Chasm.

138A

214

"whitehall"

Green End Ave.

Third Beach Rd.

St. Columba's Chapel

Indian Ave.

Bridge to NEWPORT

Paradise Ave.

Hanging Rock Rd.

Look sharp! Turn left at Tuckerman.

Tuckerman

Purgatory Chasm parking area

Sign: "2nd and Third Beaches"

138 at Sandy Point Road, Indian Avenue to Newport, 8 miles
Paradise Avenue, Green End and Third Beach Road, 2.3 miles

Indian Avenue to Hanging Rock and Purgatory Chasm
The stone, vine-covered St. Columba's Chapel sits picturesquely in the graveyard along Indian Avenue. Massive trees shade the unusually handsome gravestones and well-clipped lawn. I admired the exquisite lettering of a master stone-cutter on many of the monuments.

St. Columba's Chapel

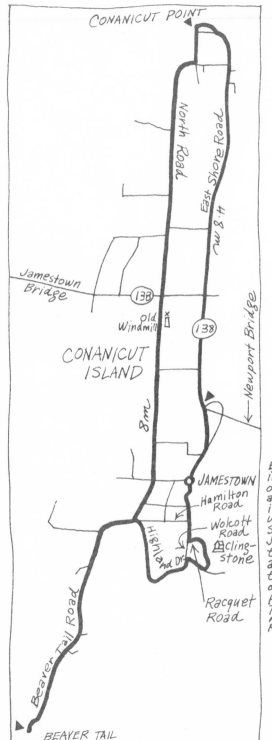

CONANICUT POINT

North Road

East Shore Road

rw 8.H

Jamestown Bridge

(138)

Old Windmill

(138)

Newport Bridge

CONANICUT ISLAND

8 m

JAMESTOWN

Hamilton Road

Wolcott Road

Clingstone

Highland Dr.

Racquet Road

Beaver Tail Road

BEAVER TAIL

East of the intersection of Wolcott and Highland is Fort Weatherill State Park. Just opposite the entrance a road leads to the view of Clingstone House. Note: There was no marker for Racquet Road.

Conanicut Point to Beaver Tail

It is exciting to see the sea crashing ashore at Beaver Tail during a full storm, I was told. There is also the ancient windmill to view along the way, as noted on the map.

Built on a rock in Jamestown Harbor around the turn of the century is the unusual and aptly named, "Clingstone House."

Clingstone House, Jamestown Harbor

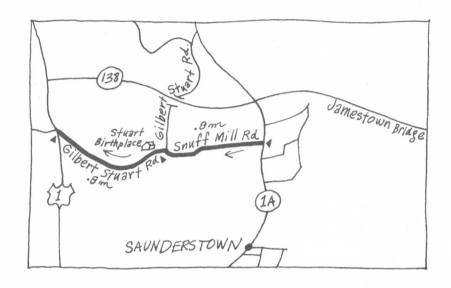

Roads to Gilbert Stuart Birthplace and Snuff Mill

In 1753 the first snuff mill in New England was erected by Gilbert Stuart's father at the head of the Mattatucket River near Saunderstown. Here, in 1755, Stuart was born, to become in later years the most distinguished of American portraitists, particularly because of his portraits of George Washington.

Buttercups

Birthplace of Gilbert Stuart near Saunderstown

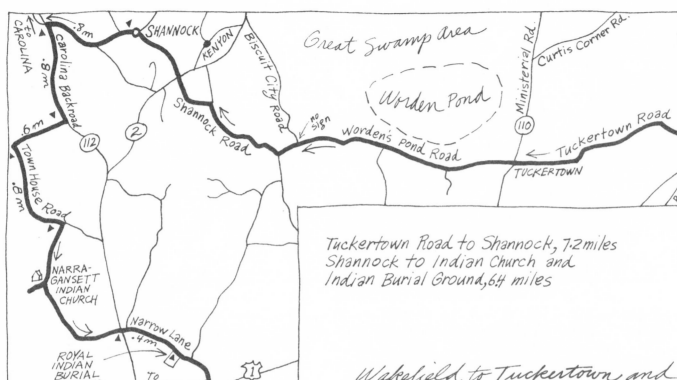

Tuckertown Road to Shannock, 7.2 miles
Shannock to Indian Church and
Indian Burial Ground, 6.4 miles

Coming from the southwest take the Wakefield turnoff off Highway 1. Go 3/10 mile to Tuckertown Road. From the North turn into Wakefield and go through town until Tuckertown Road appears on the right. Pass Worden Pond and cross Highway 2 to Shannock. Follow Old Mill Road off Highway 112, Town House and Indian Church Roads to bring you to the church and Indian Burial Ground. Note: The Narragansett church is not visible from the road. Turn in to see it. From Charlestown Narrow Lane begins about 8/10 mile northeast off Highway 1. There is a small Indian Burial Ground marker identifying it.

Wakefield to Tuckertown and Shannock

At Shannock cows ambled down the road and across the bridge over the Pawcatuck River. Some boys came canoeing from Worden Pond, stopped to see what I was drawing, and then portaged around the horseshoe falls. In 1870 this was a mill town with S. P. Clark manufacturing cotton warps and George Weeden making plaid linsey. Today, except for the roar of the falls, it seems a quiet, country village.

Horseshoe falls, Pawcatuck River, Shannock

Narragansett Indian Church, Indian Cedar Swamp

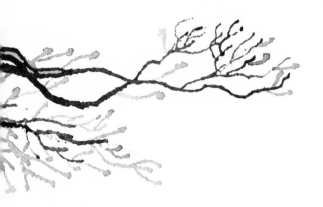

Shannock to Indian Church and
Royal Burying Grounds

   The forest surrounded
Narragansett Indian Church. Peering in the
window I noticed that the attendance
roster at the last service was "8".
 There was a small pipe organ and a
pot-bellied stove in the middle of the room.
 I made my drawing from the meadow in front
 of the church and at one point almost
dropped my pen as five motorcyclists came
roaring past me out of the woods shattering
the profound silence of the place.

Brambles

Across Rhode Island on the Back Roads

All that remains standing in West Greenwich Center is the Town Meeting House, dating from 1750. Northward along the road toward Hopkins Hollow, is the old Tillinghast property. I sat in the meadow and drew the red barn. On the left, under the trees, is one of seven cemeteries on the present 1500-acre property, which is privately owned. There were several Tillinghasts buried here, behind the barn, the latest grave marked 1903.

Long ago this same area consisted of 27 farms, testimony to the fact that this part of Rhode Island, as indeed, all of New England, was once the province of the small farmer.

Now, forests grow between many of the old stone walls instead of crops.

The old Tillinghast barn, near Greene

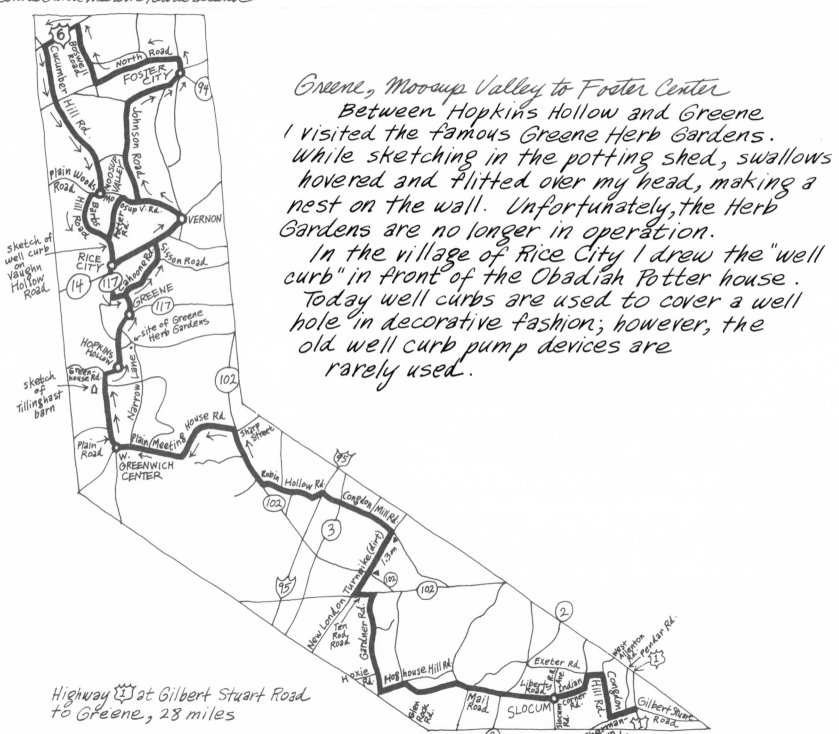

Greene, Moosup Valley to Foster Center

Between Hopkins Hollow and Greene I visited the famous Greene Herb Gardens. While sketching in the potting shed, swallows hovered and flitted over my head, making a nest on the wall. Unfortunately, the Herb Gardens are no longer in operation.

In the village of Rice City I drew the "well curb" in front of the Obadiah Potter house. Today well curbs are used to cover a well hole in decorative fashion; however, the old well curb pump devices are rarely used.

Highway 1 at Gilbert Stuart Road to Greene, 28 miles

YEARS MATURE INTO FRUIT SO THAT SOME SMALL SEEDS OF MOMENTS MAY OUTLIVE THEM   TAGORE

WORms at work
Making Soil

Nothing
Leaves
the
Land

For
Goodness
Sake
plant
Comfrey
near your
compost

Breene Herb Gardens potting shed, Greene

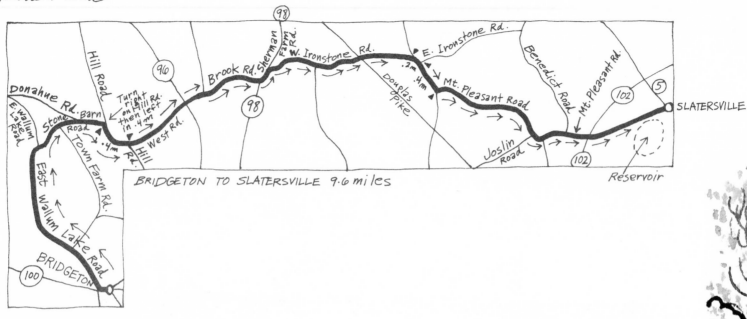

BRIDGETON TO SLATERSVILLE 9.6 miles

Back Roads to Slatersville

Mt. Pleasant country road leads past the Hutnak barn. Eighty-one-year-old Mr. Hutnak, who is Czechoslovakian-born, admitted to me that the old barn needed fixing but had good, strong, heavy timber inside. I asked him if he knew when it was constructed. He answered, smiling: "I don't know, maybe Columbus built it."

Farm on Mt. Pleasant Road near Slatersville

Well curb, Obadiah Potter House, 1804, Rice City.

Connecticut

It is interesting to see along the way the many millponds of Connecticut and imagine the picturesque waterwheels that once turned in the streams. They varied in size from those of big cotton mills to the waterwheel of a single-owner farm.

Almost every road in the areas of Connecticut explored in the following pages led to historic places, pleasant villages, and friendly people.

Wild Lily of the Valley

• MONTEREY

MASSACHUSETTS

• CANAAN

• NORFOLK

NORTH • WOODSTOCK   • NORTH
                       GROSVENOR
              • WOODSTOCK   DALE
              SOUTH
              WOODSTOCK
• FALLS   • WESTFORD
  VILLAGE   EASTFORD   POMFRET
                    • WILLINGTON

• SHARON
         • CORNWALL   BROOKLYN
              • GOSHEN   WAUREGAN
    CORNWALL • MILTON
    BRIDGE
• KENT FURNACE   • LITCHFIELD
• KENT   WINDHAM
                                  HANOVER   • HOPEVILLE
         • WASHINGTON DEPOT   JEWETT
         • JUDDS BRIDGE   CITY

                                                      NORTH
• LANESVILLE   STONINGTON

RHODE ISLAND

• MOOSUP
  VALLEY,
  R.I.

ROCKVILLE, R.I.

Connecticut

Yawgoog Road out of Rockville, Rhode Island
Yawgoog becomes Green Fall Road upon entering
Connecticut. It was, to me, quite a lovely forest byway.
From Hopeville, back roads parallel Highway 201 to
North Stonington. Here, where the Shunock River passes
through town and under Limpert's barn, I stopped to sketch.
Note: A waterwheel and structure connecting barn and
house have been added since the drawing was made.

Shunock River, North Stonington

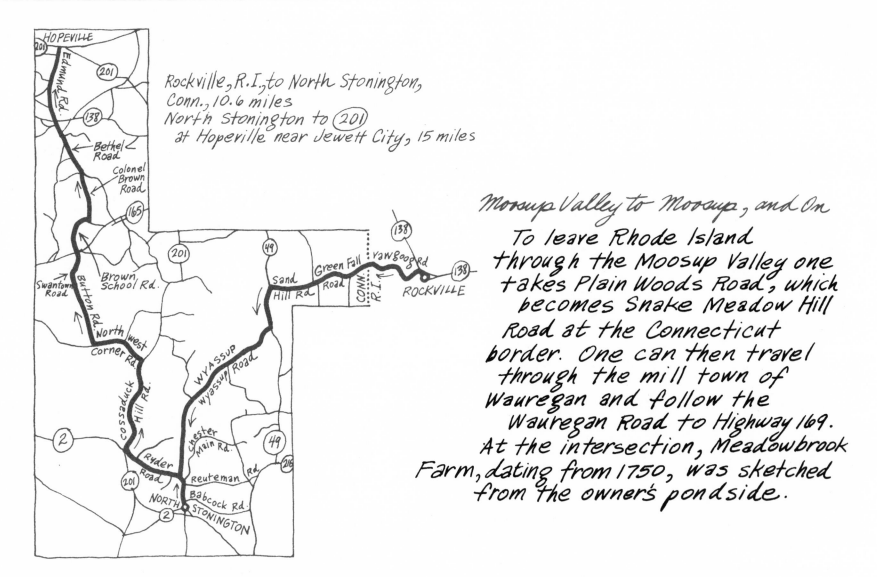

Rockville, R.I., to North Stonington,
Conn., 10.6 miles
North Stonington to (201)
   at Hopeville near Jewett City, 15 miles

Moosup Valley to Moosup, and On

To leave Rhode Island
through the Moosup Valley one
takes Plain Woods Road, which
becomes Snake Meadow Hill
Road at the Connecticut
border. One can then travel
through the mill town of
Wauregan and follow the
Wauregan Road to Highway 169.
At the intersection, Meadowbrook
Farm, dating from 1750, was sketched
from the owner's pond side.

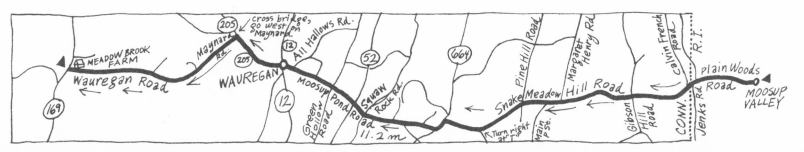

Meadowbrook Farm, Canterbury

Wedgewood Mill, Jewett City

Stetson Corner to Jewett City

These back roads led to Jewett City
and a drawing in town of the old
Slater Mill to the accompaniment
of the thundering falls close by.
The book "Griswold, a History"
mentions Slater's construction...
"In 1846 the old wooden mill was
removed and a fine brick mill of
greatly increased capacity
was erected."
An eight-year-old boy joined
me to fish for trout. Here are some
of his comments: "caught a four-pound
rainbow trout here once... giant carp
hide in the dark places. If I caught
one it'd pull me in... a muskrat
lives under the archway. He's as big
as a seal. He likes melon seeds."

apple blossoms

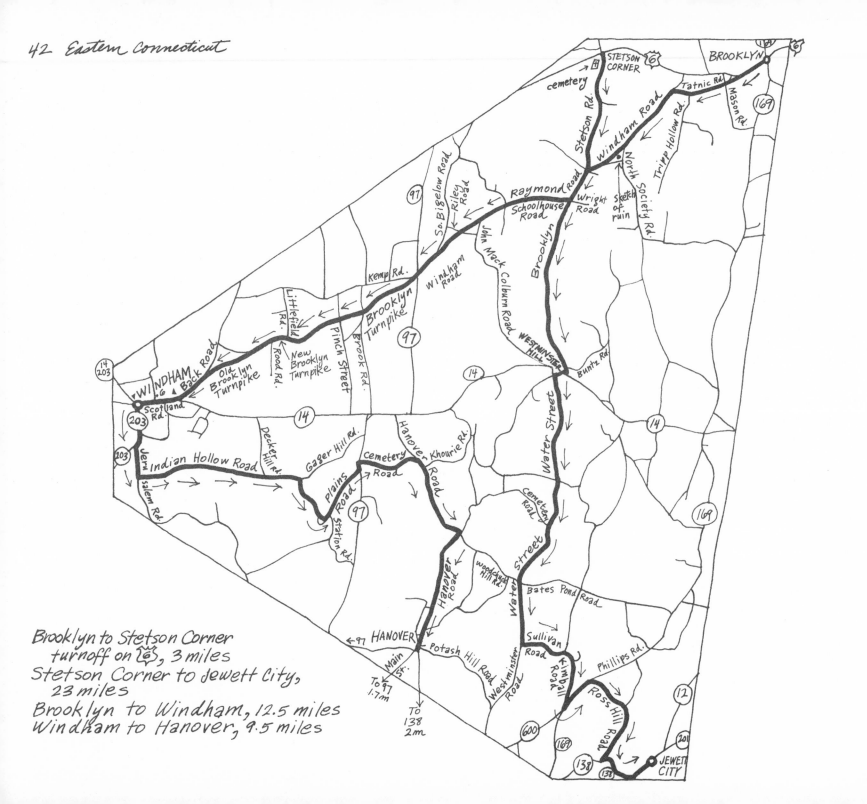

Brooklyn to Stetson Corner
turnoff on 6, 3 miles
Stetson Corner to Jewett City,
23 miles
Brooklyn to Windham, 12.5 miles
Windham to Hanover, 9.5 miles

Note: Trees and shrubs have grown in the years since the drawing was made, and the ruin is becoming difficult to see.

Ruin near Brooklyn

Brooklyn to Windham

At Windham Road and North Society Road is a stone house ruin. I was told that the roof had blown off in the hurricane of 1938. In looking at it today one can study the pioneers' use of stone in the erection of a house wall. This can be done only from the road as the property is privately owned. I was told by the owner that in the fall, somewhat to his dismay, camera enthusiasts cannot resist clambering on and photographing the ruin nestled as it is amongst the colorful maple tree foliage.

Windham to Hanover

Windham and many villages like Windham
have the perplexing problem of just too
many roads meeting at the town common.
In this otherwise lovely spot, the
clamorous and continuous sound of
trucks and cars grunting and squealing,
shifting and accelerating, seems
out of place.

Windham

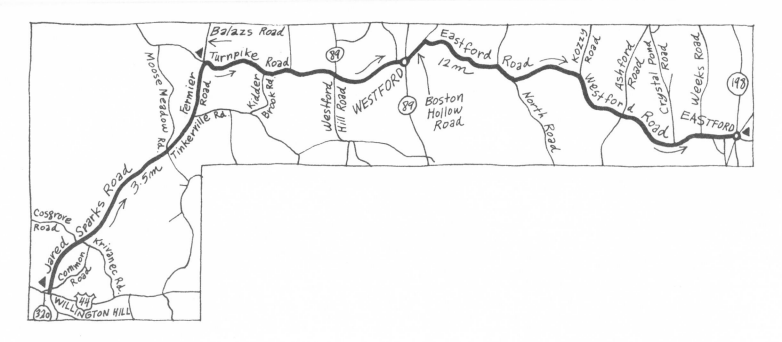

Bluets

Jared Sparks Road, Westford to Eastford

On Boston Hollow Road, Westford, is the Hazen house, also known as the old Barlow Home, now over 200 years old. The addition on the left was once the village store. As I sketched, an unmistakable and most pleasant aroma drifted past my nostrils. Mrs. Hazen was baking apple pies!

The old Barlow home, Westford

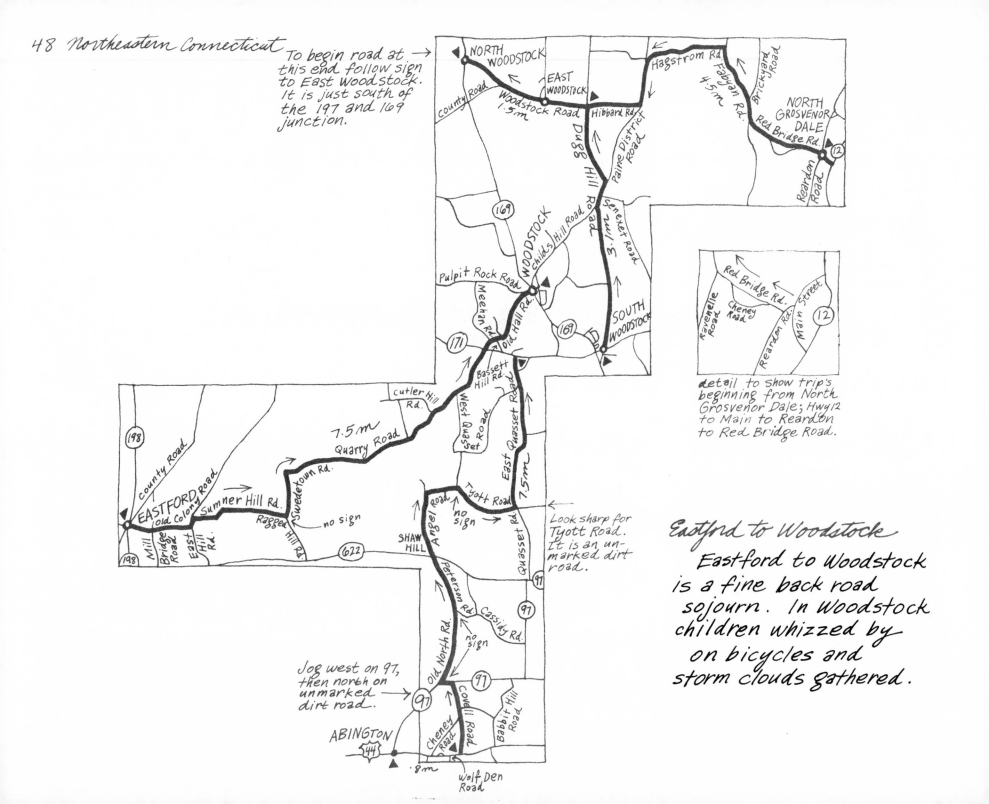

To begin road at this end follow sign to East Woodstock. It is just south of the 197 and 169 junction.

NORTH WOODSTOCK

EAST WOODSTOCK

Hagstrom Rd.

Brickyard Road

NORTH GROSVENOR DALE

County Road

Woodstock Road 1.5 m

Hibbard Rd.

Paine District Road

Fabyan Rd. 4.5 m

Red Bridge Rd.

Dugg Hill Road

Reardon Road

12

169

WOODSTOCK

Childs Hill Road

Senexet Road 3 m.

Pulpit Rock Road

Meehan Rd.

Old Hall Rd.

169

SOUTH WOODSTOCK

171

Bassett Hill Rd.

West Quasset Road

East Quasset Road

Red Bridge Rd.

Cheney Road

Ravenelle Road

Reardon Rd.

Main Street

12

detail to show trip's beginning from North Grosvenor Dale; Hwy 12 to Main to Reardon to Red Bridge Road.

Cutler Hill Rd.

198

County Road

EASTFORD

Old Colony Road

7.5 m Quarry Road

Swedetown Rd.

Sumner Hill Rd.

no sign

Ragged Hill Rd.

East Hill Rd.

Mill Bridge Road

198

622

SHAW HILL

Angel Road

Tyott Road

no sign

Quasset Rd.

East Quasset Road 7.5 m

Look sharp for Tyott Road. It is an unmarked dirt road.

Peterson Rd.

Cassidy Rd.

no sign

97

97

Old North Rd.

Jog west on 97, then north on unmarked dirt road.

97

ABINGTON

44

Cheney Road

Covell Road

Babbit Hill Road

97

Wolf Den Road

.8 m

Eastford to Woodstock

Eastford to Woodstock is a fine back road sojourn. In Woodstock children whizzed by on bicycles and storm clouds gathered.

Church on the common, Woodstock

Three Roads to East Woodstock

My walk in the graveyard was especially
rewarding, for beside one memorial grew
two mature asparagus. Harvesting them
reverently, they proved most tender and
sweet at the evening meal.

Road to East Woodstock

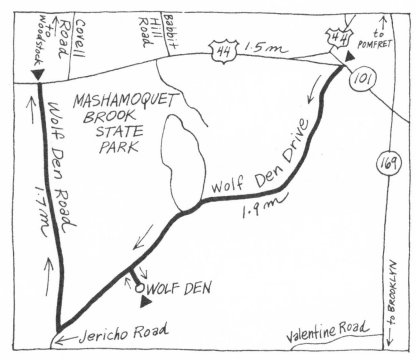

Note: First you reach
Mashamoquet Brook State Park
Campgrounds on Wolf
Den Drive. In 1.8 miles
there is a "walk-in"
entrance to Wolf Den
followed by the "drive-
in" entrance shortly
thereafter.

Yellow
Mustard

Wolf Den Road

Along this forest road
in Mashamoquet
Brook State Park you
can park conveniently
and hike to see
the lair of the last
sheep-killing wolf in
Connecticut. Israel
Putnam shot him,
deep in the den,
in 1742.

Israel Putnam Wolf Den, near Pomfret

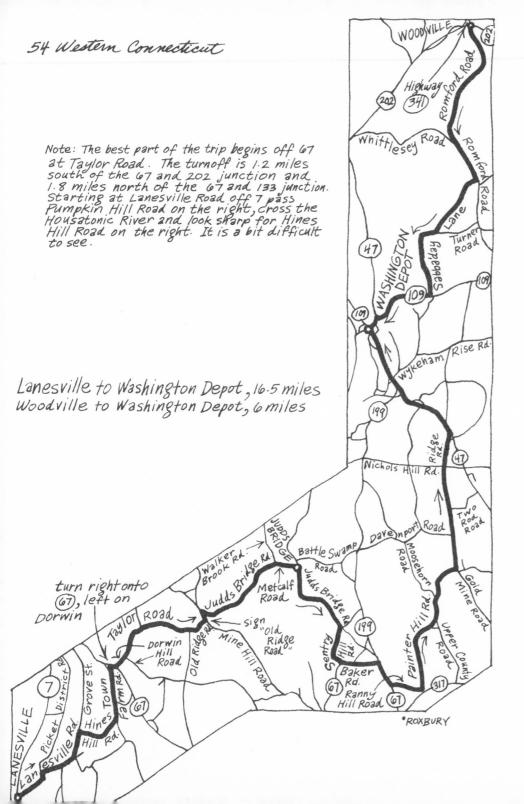

Note: The best part of the trip begins off 67 at Taylor Road. The turnoff is 1.2 miles south of the 67 and 202 junction and 1.8 miles north of the 67 and 133 junction. Starting at Lanesville Road off 7 pass Pumpkin Hill Road on the right, cross the Housatonic River and look sharp for Hines Hill Road on the right. It is a bit difficult to see.

Lanesville to Washington Depot, 16.5 miles
Woodville to Washington Depot, 6 miles

Meandering to Washington Depot

Up and down hills, on paved and dirt roads, through the green, green forests of New Milford, Roxbury, and Washington townships one finally emerges at Highway 47 and Washington Depot. As I sketched there, boys canoed expertly down the rushing Shepaug River.

Washington Depot

Roads to Litchfield

Any road to Litchfield, with its many fine colonial mansions, is a pleasure to drive. I couldn't decide which historic house to draw and, as you see, instead sketched this more modest, but colorful old brick building in the shopping area of town.

Marsh Blue Violets

Phelps Block Shops, Litchfield

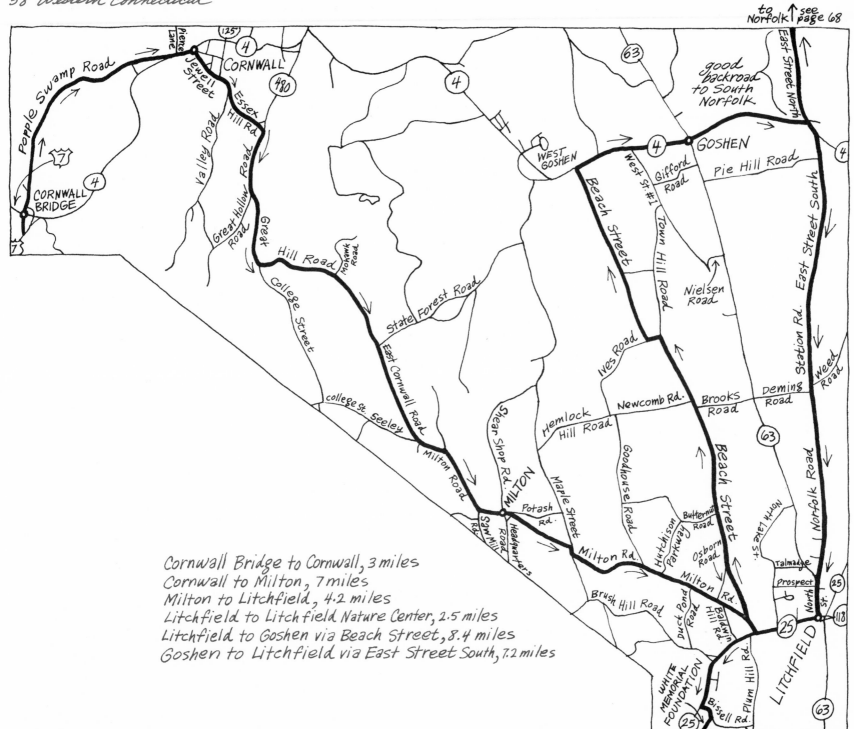

to Norfolk ↑ see page 68

Cornwall Bridge to Cornwall, 3 miles
Cornwall to Milton, 7 miles
Milton to Litchfield, 4.2 miles
Litchfield to Litchfield Nature Center, 2.5 miles
Litchfield to Goshen via Beach Street, 8.4 miles
Goshen to Litchfield via East Street South, 7.2 miles

Southwest of Litchfield

At the White Memorial Foundation's Nature Center were two live screech owls. When I got too close to them one would "clack" his bill and the other make a cricketlike sound. Children were touring through the center as I drew and I received a supreme compliment from one who said, "You draw better than our art teacher!"

Screech Owls, Litchfield Nature Center

Trinity Episcopal Church, 1802, Milton

Cornwall Bridge, Cornwall, and Milton to Litchfield

Big, tall white pine grow in the Nature Conservancy sanctuary along Essex Hill Road. Some seemingly grow from the rock itself.
No one came by as I sketched the old church in Milton. It seemed a quiet village, indeed.
From here a delightful country road proceeds to Litchfield.

White pine and
rock, Essex Hill Road

Goshen to Litchfield

The big, bright golden eagle distinguishes the Goshen Historical Society building. In the early days this was Eagle Academy, where students could prepare for entrance into Yale University.

Kent Furnace to West Cornwall

The superb Sloane-Stanley Museum of early farm implements begins this back road route through Macedonia Brook State Park to Sharon and West Cornwall.

Where Macedonia Brook Road branches into unmarked Keeler and Weber Roads, follow sign to Cornwall and Skiff Mountain.

The big eagle, Goshen Historical Society

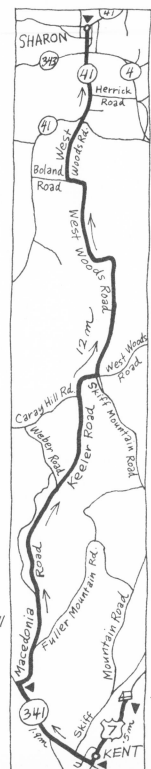

PENN. GOOSE-WING
1760

NEW ENGLAND FLARED
Broad axe
1790

N.Y. OVAL BLADE
broad axe
c. 1820

BARK SPUDS
c. 1760

R.R. TIE BROAD AXE

VERMONT SQUARED
broad axe

SCORING AXE

TRUNNEL MALLET

TRUNNELS (Tree Nails)

"Wheelbarrows were works of art", Sloane-Stanley Museum, Kent Furnace

The falls, near Falls Village

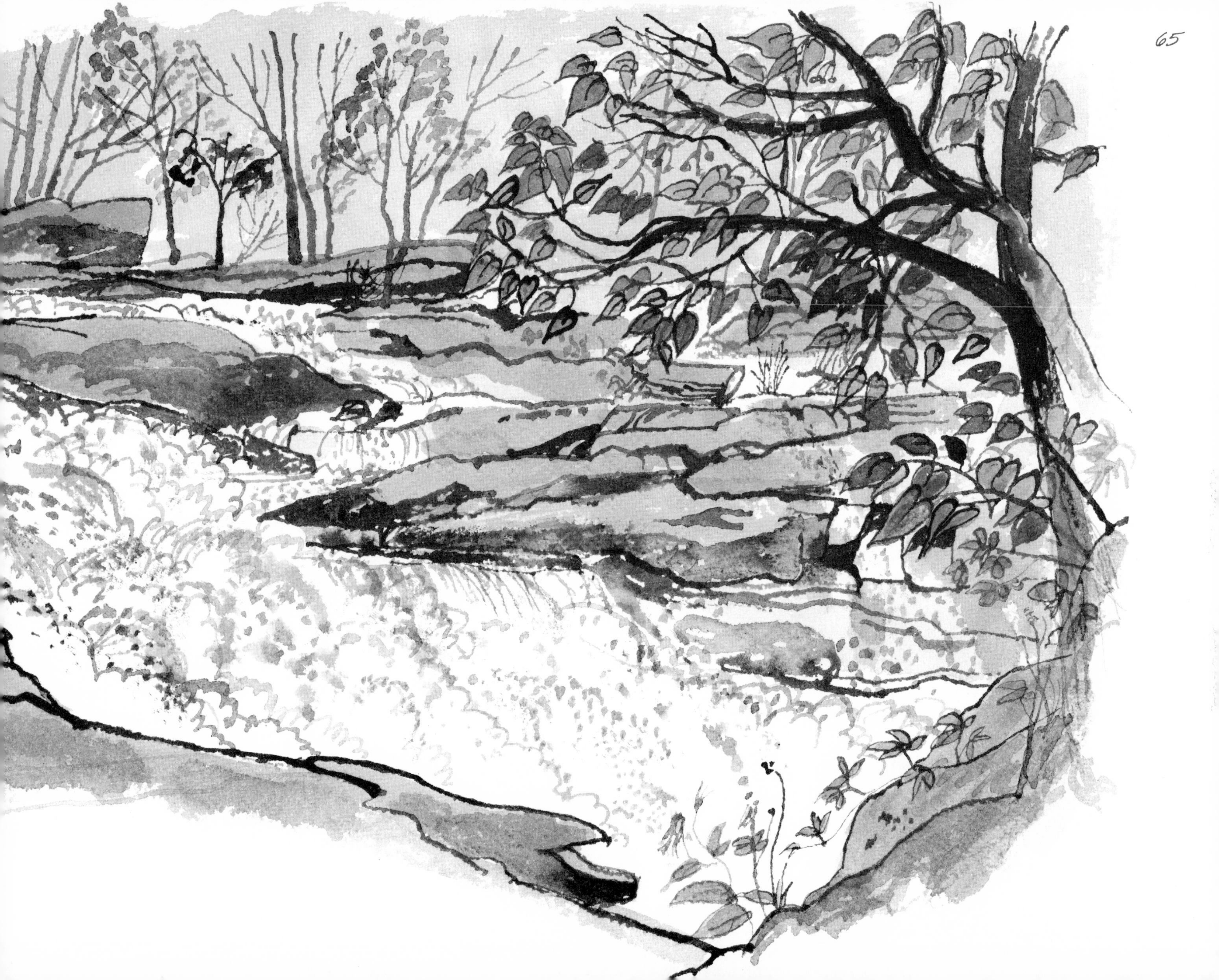

Twin Lakes Road to Bartholomew's Cobble. ↓ See map, page 74. ↓

River Road from West Cornwall

The Housatonic River is right beside you on this road out of West Cornwall. Sometimes trees make a canopy overhead. Just north of Falls Village is an overlook of the great, tumbling falls themselves.

Northern Bush Honeysuckle

WEST CORNWALL

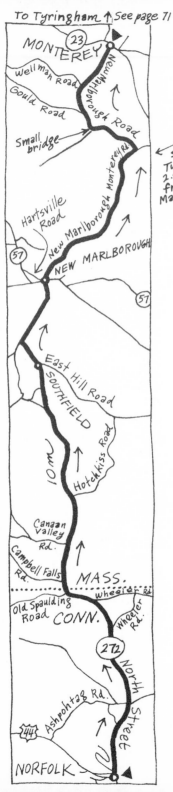

To Tyringham ↑ See page 71

MONTEREY (23)

Wellman Road

Gould Road

Small bridge

Newmarlborough Road

← no sign.. Turn left 2.9 miles from New Marlborough

Hartsville Road

New Marlborough Monterey Rd.

(51)

NEW MARLBOROUGH

(57)

East Hill Road

SOUTHFIELD

10w

Hotchkiss Road

Canaan Valley Rd.

Campbell Falls Rd.

MASS.

Wheeler Rd.

Old Spaulding Road CONN.

Wheeler Rd.

(272)

North Street

Ashpohtag Rd.

(44)

NORFOLK

Norfolk to Monterey

The charming town of Norfolk, home of the Yale Summer Music Program, has a splendid Victorian fountain designed by the well-known architect of his time, Stanford White. It serves drinking water to local and itinerant birds, horses, and dogs, and I also observed mortals on bicycles drink from the bird dish spout.

ERECTED AD MDCCLXXXIX

MEMORY OF JOSEPH BATTEL NORFOLK 1806 1874.

Fountain on the common, Norfolk

Massachusetts

Massachusetts has a fascinating network of back roads so extensive that one could fill many books such as this with travel suggestions. My report is mainly concerned with western Massachusetts, an area of great beauty, indeed. I feel that I must congratulate the people of this state and all of New England wherever churches are kept painted, graveyards clipped, historic houses restored, and "progress" resisted whenever it endangered beauty, health, and the preservation of America's historical sites and structures.

Lesser Stitchwort

NORTHFIELD •

• ROYALSTON • WINCHENDON   WEST TOWNSEND

• ASHBURNHAM

ADAMS •

GREENFIELD •

• WENDELL   • ATHOL
  DEPOT

CHESHIRE •

LANESBORO •

CONWAY •   • DEERFIELD

• PHILLIPSTON

WEST WHATELY •   • SOUTH DEERFIELD

• PETERSHAM

• PITTSFIELD

HATFIELD •

• BOLTON

HANCOCK
• SHAKER VILLAGE

SUDBURY •

• LENOX
• WEST STOCKBRIDGE
  • LEE

Massachusetts

• STOCKBRIDGE

• ALFORD   • TYRINGHAM
• NORTH EGREMONT
• SOUTH EGREMONT   • MONTEREY

• SHEFFIELD

• ASHLEY FALLS

Road to Tyringham

Tyringham is a lovely, green valley enclosed on three sides by mountains. Mark Twain knew this area in his time and in the summer artists, writers, and musicians still come to live in the valley.

From 1792 to 1894 Tyringham was the site of a large Shaker settlement, and many of their homes hereabouts are still in use.

Tyringham Galleries occupy the "Gingerbread House," built in the 30s to the bizarre taste of sculptor, Henry Kitson.

PROVINCETOWN ●

● PLYMOUTH

● WESTPORT FACTORY

"Gingerbread House," Tyringham

From ⟨44⟩, Weotogue Road to
Bartholomew's Cobble, 3.7 miles
Ashley Falls to ⟨7⟩ at Brookside
Road, 10 miles

Gill-over-
the-ground

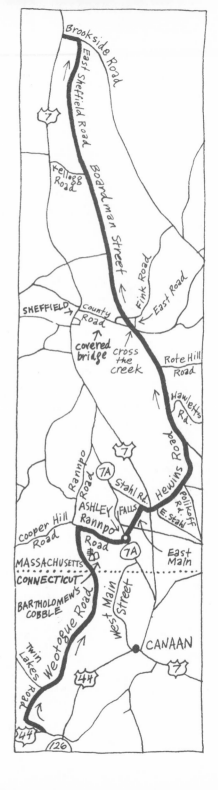

Weotogue Road and Bartholomew's Cobble

Weotogue Road and its farms and pastures, meadows and river views passes Bartholomew's Cobble, an area preserved for man in all its infinite beauty. The late Mark Van Doren wrote of the Cobble in 1970, "a little marble mountain upon whose sides grow trees of ancient origin and plants of unimaginable age. May nothing ever threaten its serenity."

Sheffield to South Egremont
to Stockbridge

This is a wonderful collection of farm and forest back roads. In Alford, along the way, stop to walk among the tall graveyard monuments. There was a bit of competition, I imagine, as to whose stone memorial would be highest.

Egremont Town Hall, 1822

Included in this drawing of Stockbridge's colorful main street is Norman Rockwell's old studio, with its second-story picture window.

Stockbridge

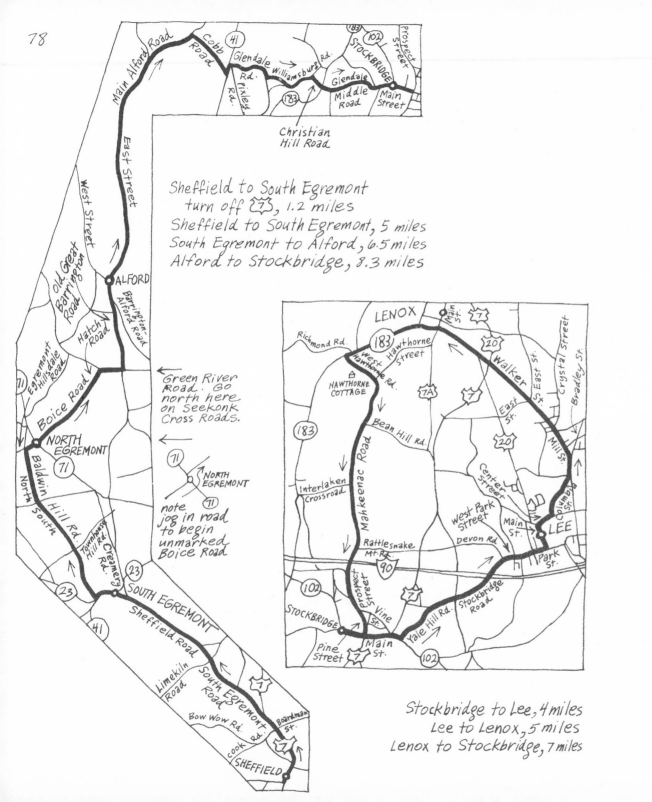

Main Alford Road
Cobb Road
41
Glendale Rd.
Williamsburg Rd.
Pixley Rd.
183
102
Prospect Street
STOCKBRIDGE
Glendale Middle Road
Main Street
Christian Hill Road

East Street
West Street

Sheffield to South Egremont
turn off ⑦, 1.2 miles
Sheffield to South Egremont, 5 miles
South Egremont to Alford, 6.5 miles
Alford to Stockbridge, 8.3 miles

Old Great Barrington Road
ALFORD
Barrington-Alford Road
Hatch Road

Egremont-Hillsdale Road
71

Boice Road

→ Green River Road. Go north here on Seekonk Cross Roads.

NORTH EGREMONT
71

71
NORTH EGREMONT
71
note jog in road to begin unmarked Boice Road

Baldwin
North South Hill Rd.
71

Townhouse Hill Rd.
Creamery Rd.
23

23
SOUTH EGREMONT
41

Sheffield Road
South Egremont Road
Limekiln Road
Bow Wow Rd.
cook Rd.
Boardman St.
⑦
SHEFFIELD

LENOX
Main St.
7
Richmond Rd.
183
Hawthorne Street
West Hawthorne Rd.
20
Walker St.
East St.
Crystal Street
Bradley St.
HAWTHORNE COTTAGE
7A
7
183
Bean Hill Rd.
East St.
Mahkeenac Road
20
Center Street
Mill St.
Interlaken Crossroad
West Park Street
Columbia St.
Main St.
LEE
Rattlesnake Mt. Rd.
Devon Rd.
Park St.
90
102
Prospect Street
Vine St.
7
Yale Hill Rd.
Stockbridge Road
STOCKBRIDGE
Pine Street
7
Main St.
102

Stockbridge to Lee, 4 miles
Lee to Lenox, 5 miles
Lenox to Stockbridge, 7 miles

Edgewood Farm near Lee

Stockbridge Loop

Along Yale Hill Road one dewy morning I sketched this barn. The road leads directly into the paper-mill town of Lee, with its big white church on the common. I traveled Walker Street to Lenox and then back past Lake Mahkeenac to Stockbridge.

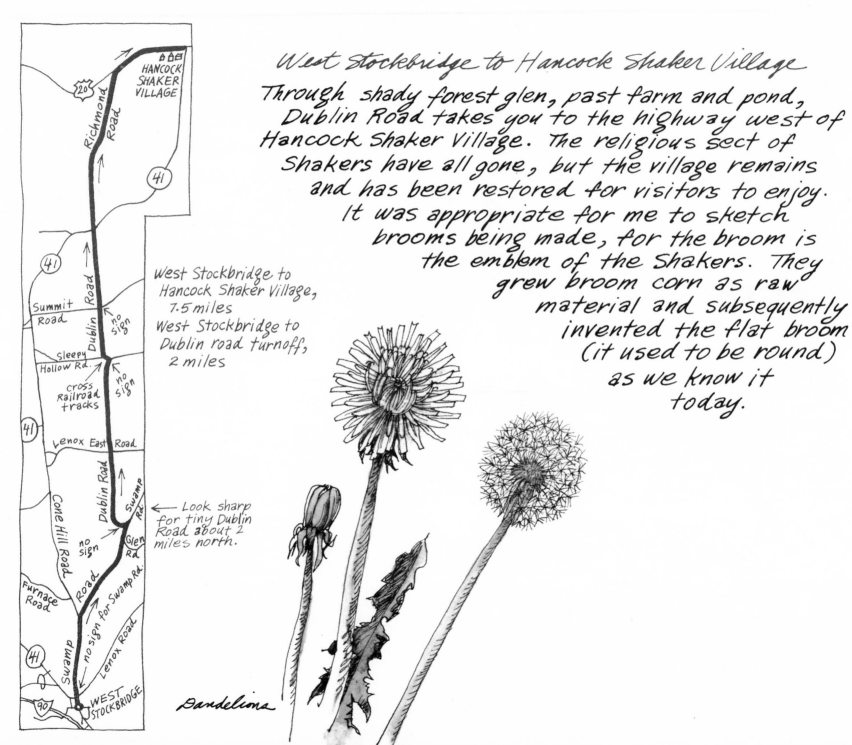

West Stockbridge to Hancock Shaker Village,
7.5 miles

West Stockbridge to Dublin road turnoff,
2 miles

← Look sharp for tiny Dublin Road about 2 miles north.

West Stockbridge to Hancock Shaker Village

Through shady forest glen, past farm and pond, Dublin Road takes you to the highway west of Hancock Shaker Village. The religious sect of Shakers have all gone, but the village remains and has been restored for visitors to enjoy. It was appropriate for me to sketch brooms being made, for the broom is the emblem of the Shakers. They grew broom corn as raw material and subsequently invented the flat broom (it used to be round) as we know it today.

Dandelions

Broom vises, Hancock Shaker Village

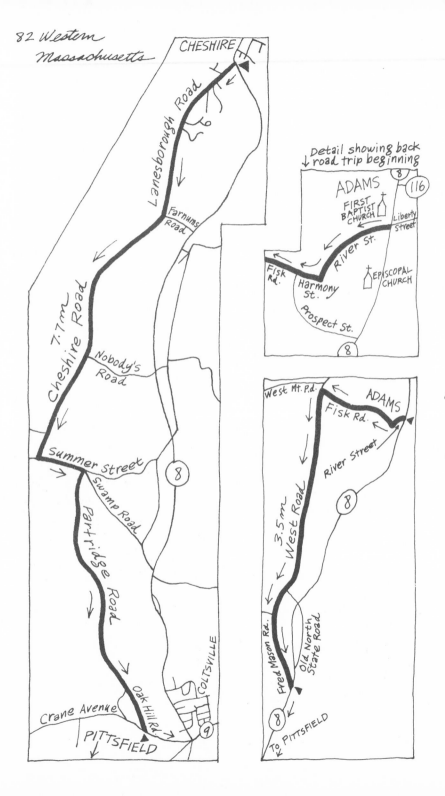

CHESHIRE

Lanesborough Road

Farnums Road

7.7m

Cheshire Road

Nobody's Road

Summer Street

Swamp Road

Partridge Road

Crane Avenue

Oak Hill Rd.

COLTSVILLE

PITTSFIELD

8

9

Detail showing back
↓ road trip beginning

ADAMS

8

116

FIRST BAPTIST CHURCH

Liberty Street

River St.

Fisk Rd.

Harmony St.

EPISCOPAL CHURCH

Prospect St.

8

West Mt. Rd.

ADAMS

Fisk Rd.

River Street

3.5m West Road

Fred Mason Rd.

Old North State Road

8

8

To Pittsfield

Adams to Pittsfield

From Adams off Highway 8 there is a country road south that begins at River Road, just south of the First Baptist Church. Where the road returns to Route 8 again you can travel on it south and exit at Lanesborough Road, which will again permit a tranquil pace to Pittsfield.

Farm on Fred Mason Road, Cheshire

Williamsburg to Conway

Forest scenery, babbling brooks, and a good
dirt road from West Whately bring you down
the hill to Conway. Approaching
a village such as this on a
country road, I've found, helps

Covered Bridge,
Conway

To see this view take Hill View and
turn west on Orchard Street. There is
no more dust. The street has been paved.

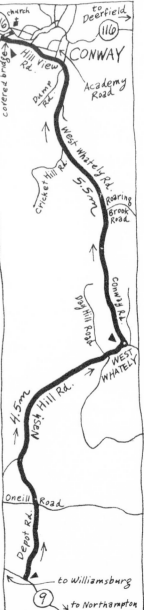

give one an even greater sense
of the history of the town.
I was brought out of my horse
and buggy reverie somewhat
as occasional autos and trucks
using the covered bridge I was
sketching passed and layered
me with dust. I mused that
horses and buggies would have
done the same.

Conway to Deerfield

In the most beautiful
village of Deerfield, from
1732 to 1780, Reverend
Jonathan Ashley, preacher
and "Tory", resided behind
this unpainted, marvelously
weathered door.

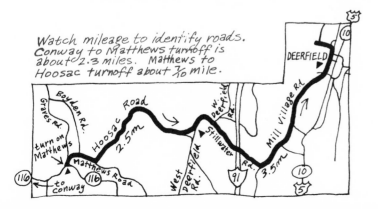

Watch mileage to identify roads.
Conway to Matthews turnoff is
about 2.3 miles. Matthews to
Hoosac turnoff about 7/10 mile.

DEERFIELD

Graves Rd. Boyden Rd.
Hoosac Road 2.5m
turn on Matthews
116 116 Matthews Road
to Conway
West Deerfield Rd.
Stillwater Rd.
W. Deerfield Rd.
91 3.5m
Mill Village Rd.
10 5
5 10

Ashley House
entrance,
Deerfield

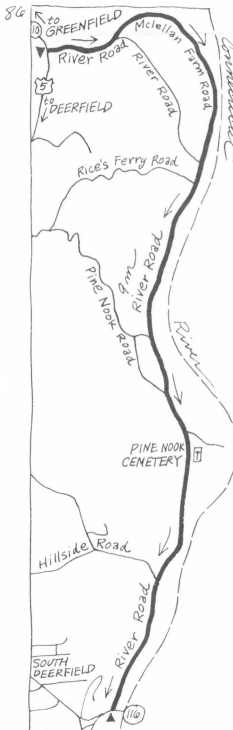

to GREENFIELD
10
River Road
Mclellan Farm Road
River Road
5
to DEERFIELD
Connecticut
Rice's Ferry Road
River Road
Pine Nook Road
Fm River Road
River
PINE NOOK CEMETERY
Hillside Road
River Road
SOUTH DEERFIELD
116

↓ For continuation of River Road see page 88.

Note: Look sharp for a dirt road to the left ¼ mile from River Road and Mclellan Farm Road intersection. If you miss this continuation of Mclellan the paved road will bring you to the train yard.

The River Road to South Deerfield

The Connecticut River is close by and farms and fields fill the landscape. I sketched at Pine Nook cemetery on the banks of the Connecticut listening to bird calls at the time of the setting sun.

PINE NOOK CEMETERY

Pine Nook Cemetery
River Road to South Deerfield

Sugarloaf Road

116 116

River Road

River Road 6.6m

Main Street

Pilvinis Road

Old Farms Path

Basin Rd.

Connecticut River

Roaring Brook Co.

King St.

North St.

HATFIELD

School St.

Robin Plantain

River Road to Hatfield

Along this road are vast fields of tobacco and their attendant long curing barns. I sketched a more classic barn belonging to John Olynik. He had come from the Ukraine in 1913 and told me as I drew, "I know that barn 60 year. They want me to take top off barn. I no let them." In 1917 flood waters were four feet high in the barn. It stood firm, as it does today, made for the ages with its heavy timbers fastened together in old-fashioned mortise and tenon construction.

John Olynik barn, River Road near Hatfield

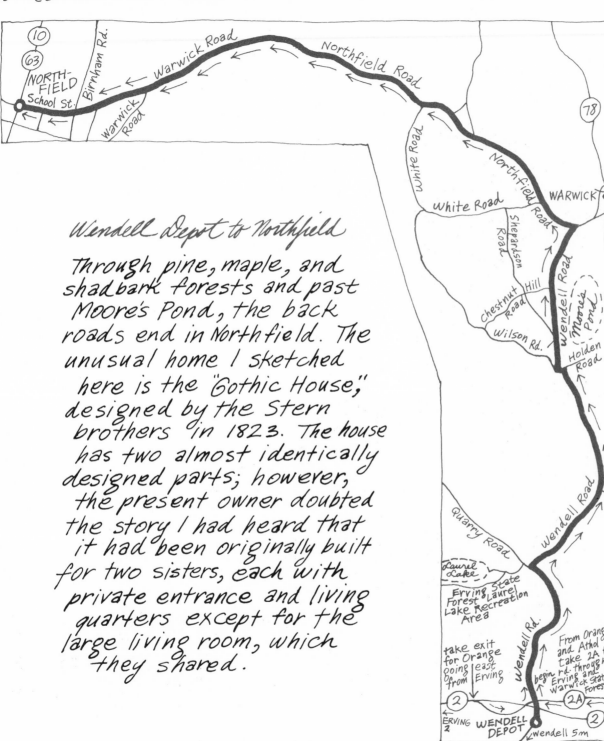

Wendell Depot to Northfield

Through pine, maple, and shadbark forests and past Moore's Pond, the back roads end in Northfield. The unusual home I sketched here is the "Gothic House," designed by the Stern brothers in 1823. The house has two almost identically designed parts; however, the present owner doubted the story I had heard that it had been originally built for two sisters, each with private entrance and living quarters except for the large living room, which they shared.

Gothic House, Northfield

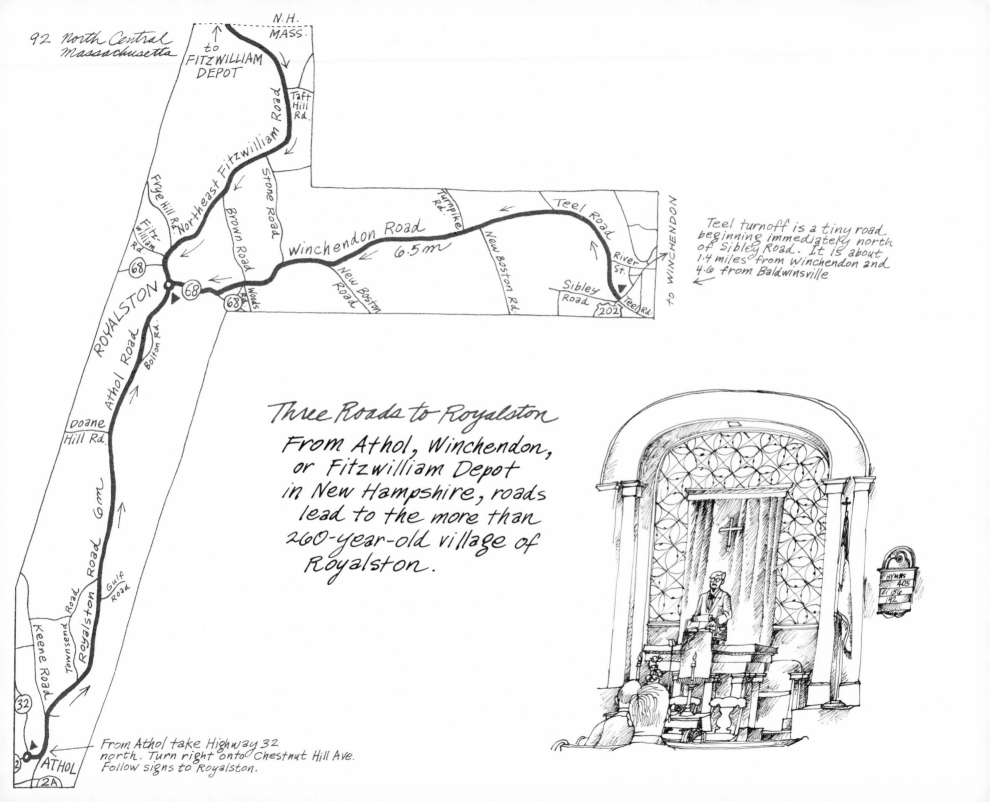

N.H.
MASS.

to FITZWILLIAM DEPOT

Taft Hill Rd.

Frye Hill Rd.

Northeast Fitzwilliam Road

Stone Road

Brown Road

Fitzwilliam Rd.

ROYALSTON

68

68

Woods

68

Turnpike Rd.

Winchendon Road 6.5m

New Boston Road

New Boston Rd.

Teel Road

to WINCHENDON

River St.

Sibley Road

Teel Rd.

202

Teel turnoff is a tiny road beginning immediately north of Sibley Road. It is about 1.4 miles from Winchendon and 4.6 from Baldwinsville

Athol Road

Bolton Rd.

Doane Hill Rd.

Royalston Road 6m

Gulf Road

Tokunut Road

Keene Road

32

Athol

2

2A

Three Roads to Royalston

From Athol, Winchendon, or Fitzwilliam Depot in New Hampshire, roads lead to the more than 260-year-old village of Royalston.

From Athol take Highway 32 north. Turn right onto Chestnut Hill Ave. Follow signs to Royalston.

HYMNS
405
156
142

It was Sunday and I not only sketched the exterior of the handsome Congregational church but also attended the service! A parishioner told me during coffee time later that there is a nest of hornets somewhere back of the chandelier and on hot, summer Sundays, these hornets in their torpor, have been known to drop on worshippers during service.

Congregational Church, 1820
Royalston

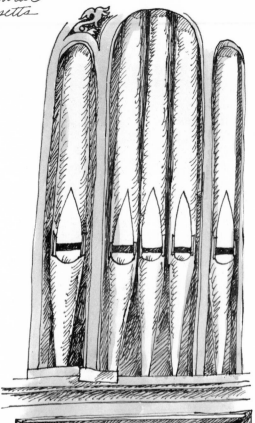

Royalston.
Congregational church organ
made by William A. Johnson, 1863

Petersham to Phillipston

Petersham country store has been
serving the community since 1840.
Only for a short period of time
was it a hat factory.
The village of Petersham, directly
south of Athol, was settled
in 1733 and named after Petersham
in Surrey, England.

Germond's
Country Store,
Petersham

Marsh Marigold

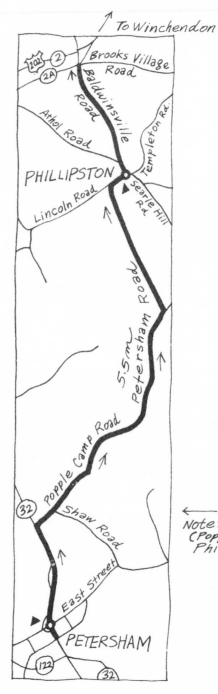

To Winchendon

202 · 2 · Brooks Village Road
2A
Baldwinsville Road
Athol Road
Templeton Rd.
PHILLIPSTON
Searle Hill Rd
Lincoln Road
5.5m. Petersham Road
Popple Camp Road
32
Shaw Road
East Street
PETERSHAM
122 · 32

Phillipston's 1785 church
has a faceless, century-
old, wooden-geared
clock in its tower.
To preserve the
precious wooden
parts an electric
striker now hits the
1840 bell in the
belfry.

← Note: Turn off 32 onto Highway 101
(Popple Camp Road). Go left at
Phillipston Center sign.

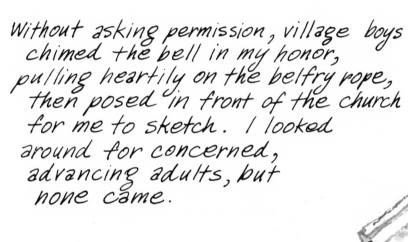

Without asking permission, village boys
chimed the bell in my honor,
pulling heartily on the belfry rope,
then posed in front of the church
for me to sketch. I looked
around for concerned,
advancing adults, but
none came.

Church of the faceless clock, Phillipston

The Way to Ashburnham

1975 marked the 100th birthday for Eclipse #2 Firehouse. A country road drive to Ashburnham starts here at New Fitchburg Road. Where South Road comes in there is a marker telling how, in the early days, Fitch (for whom the town of Fitchburg is named) and his family were kidnapped by Indians, taken to Canada and held for ransom.

Eclipse Fire Engine Company No. 2, North Townsend

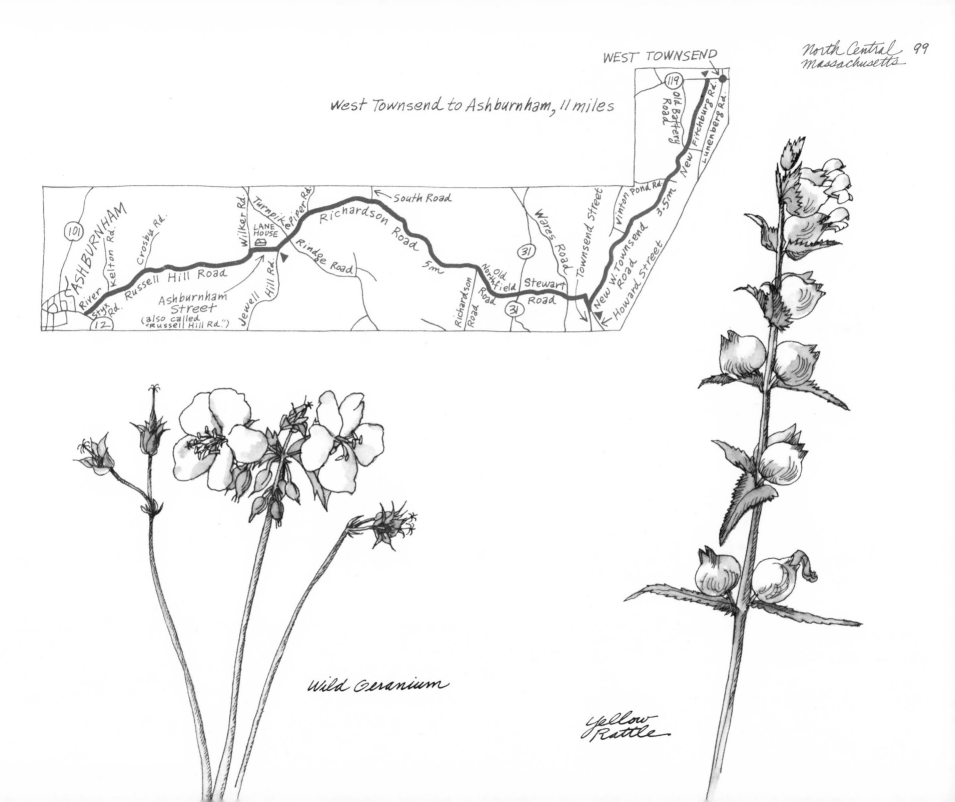

WEST TOWNSEND

West Townsend to Ashburnham, 11 miles

119

Old Battery Road

New Fitchburg Rd.

Lunenberg Rd.

ASHBURNHAM

101

River

Styx Rd.

Kelton Rd.

Crosby Rd.

Russell Hill Road

Ashburnham Street
(also called "Russell Hill Rd.")

12

Jewell Hill Rd.

Wilker Rd.

Turnpike

Piper Rd.

LANE HOUSE

Rindge Road

Richardson Road

South Road

5 m

Richardson Road

Old Northfield Road

31

Stewart Road

31

Wares Road

Townsend Street

Vinton Pond Rd.

New W. Townsend Road

3.5 m

Howard Street

Wild Geranium

Yellow Rattle

Lane House, 1810, Russell Hill Road, Ashburnham

Sudbury to Bolton

Along this way is Mrs. Meigs' house, originally colonial in design, with later additions of a Victorian style. The house is on Randall Street near the golf course and golf balls occasionally pepper the 18th-century house. Mrs. Meigs said that her cat, a skunk, and a large woodchuck spent the winter under the porch. The woodchuck even made an appearance for me while I was there.

Flowering Dogwood

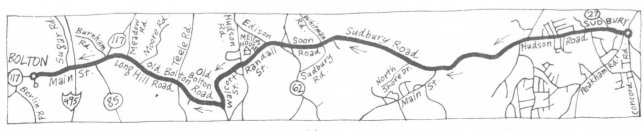

Sudbury to Bolton, 12.3 miles

Mrs. Meigs "Saltbox Victorian"

On Old Sandwich Road

I sketched Plymouth town from the yacht club
and continued south toward Cape Cod on
Old Sandwich Road, past lovely estates,
and through sometimes dense
pitch pine forests.

Plymouth

Blue-eyed grass

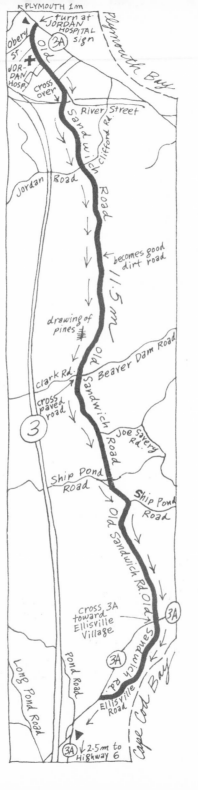

← PLYMOUTH 1m

turn at JORDAN HOSPITAL sign

3A

Obery St.

Old

cross over

River Street

Sandwich

Clifford Rd.

JORDAN Hosp.

Jordan Road

Road

becomes good dirt road

1.5 m

drawing of pines

Clark Rd.

Beaver Dam Road

cross paved road

Old Sandwich Road

3

Joe Salery Rd.

Ship Pond Road

Ship Pond Road

Old Sandwich Rd. Old

Cross 3A toward Ellisville Village

3A

Long Pond Road

Pond Road

3A

Sandwich Rd.

Ellisville Road

Plymouth Bay

Cape Cod Bay

3A ↓ 2.5m to Highway 6

Beach plum blossoms

Old Sandwich Road

BOATS & MOTORS
Fishing Tackle Beach Access

Provincetown

The Old Road to Provincetown

The old road is Cranberry Highway (Highway 6A), bypassed
today by the fast U.S. Highway 6. This is the only
"back road" in this book that is busy and highly populated;
however, the Cape towns along each coast are of infinite
interest and I wish to suggest their exploration.
Old Highway 28 and 28A and County Road can be the
basis for exploring the ocean coast on the return trip.

Vermont

Vermont is the state for back roads.
They are mostly dirt but well graded.
  In Connecticut, Massachusetts, and
Rhode Island vistas are obscured by trees,
but Vermont rewards one's eyes with open,
  rolling farm landscape and also
    picturesque views of approaching
towns. And the land seems more
    remote here from urban
      influences.

Bird's-foot Trefoil

BORDOVILLE•
FAIRFIELD•
•BELVIDERE
•CENTER

GRAND ISLE•   ST. ALBANS•
•   BAY

WEST BURKE•

WATERVILLE•
JOHNSON•

SOUTH HERO•   •WEST MILTON
SHEFFIELD•   GALLUP•
               MILLS

MORRISVILLE•
HARDWICK•

NORTH CONCORD•

SOUTH WOODBURY•   CABOT• DANVILLE•

•SHELBURNE   KENTS•
              CORNER

PEACHAM•

•CHARLOTTE   ADAMANT•

MONTPELIER•
•FERRISBURG

•VERGENNES

Vermont

•WEYBRIDGE

•MIDDLEBURY

BETHEL•
SOUTH ROYALTON•
GAYSVILLE•   SHARON•

WEST HARTFORD•
QUECHEE•
CHIPPENHOOK•   •CLARENDON
HARTLAND•

•TINMOUTH

•DANBY FOUR CORNERS
•DANBY   SPRINGFIELD•
          CHESTER•

GRAFTON•

•MANCHESTER DEPOT

•CHISELVILLE
•EAST ARLINGTOWN

•BENNINGTON

Peter Matteson Museum, 1777

Bennington to East Arlington

Lady Gosford, who liked to be called Beatrice, countess of Gosford,
bought this old tavern in 1926, and it stands today along an old
stagecoach road to East Arlington. She had named it Topping
Tavern. Today the name Peter Matteson has been restored. Peter
owned and farmed a large number of acres here in the late 1700s.
He also ran his own tavern!

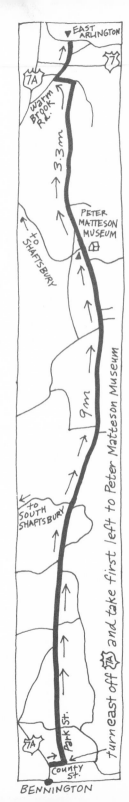

Chiselville to Manchester

Chiselville's ax head and chisel factory burned down a long time ago. The more than 100-year-old bridge still stands, but there are plans to put a "run-through vehicle arcade" a distance from either end of it so that trucks or trailers that are too large for the bridge will be warned of that fact before damaging the bridge proper.

Painted Trillium

Map labels (left map):

EAST ARLINGTON
7
7A
Warm Brook Rd.
3.3m
to SHAFTSBURY
PETER MATTESON MUSEUM
9m
to SOUTH SHAFTSBURY
turn east off 7A and take first left to Peter Matteson Museum
Park St.
7A
County St.
BENNINGTON

Map labels (right map):

MANCHESTER
7
8m
SUNDERLAND
7
SUNDERLAND STATION
to Arlington
covered bridge
CHISELVILLE
KANSAS
EAST ARLINGTON

ONE DOLLAR FINE
FOR DRIVING FASTER THAN A
WALK ON THIS BRIDGE.

Chiselville Bridge

Jack-
in-the-Pulpit

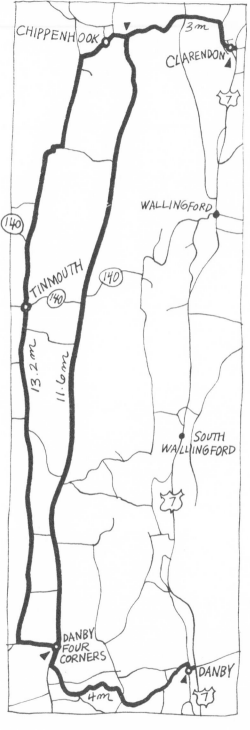

Danby to Chippenhook and Clarendon

Pearl Buck lived in Danby the
last years of her life and walked
through the village each day,
recognizable immediately by the
oriental robe she wore. The Village
Bookshop sold Pearl Buck books
almost exclusively. It is now a
private residence called Millbrook
House, circa 1800-1835.

Up the hill from Danby two
parallel back roads go north from
Danby Four Corners past farm,
forest, and mountain
scenery toward Tinmouth
and Chippenhook.

The Village Bookshop, Danby

To South Royalton and Bethel

A very interesting and meandering road along the White River takes you to South Royalton and Bethel. The horseshoe-shaped "Handy Memorial" on South Royalton's common is engraved, "In honor of Hannah Hunter Handy who rescued 9 children from the Indians at the burning of Royalton, Oct. 16, 1780, after she married Gideon Mosher of Sharon, Vt."
   Also engraved are the words, "Phineas Parkhurst who was shot at the Indian raid rode with a bullet in his side to Lebanon, New Hampshire, giving the alarm.

On the green,
South Royalton

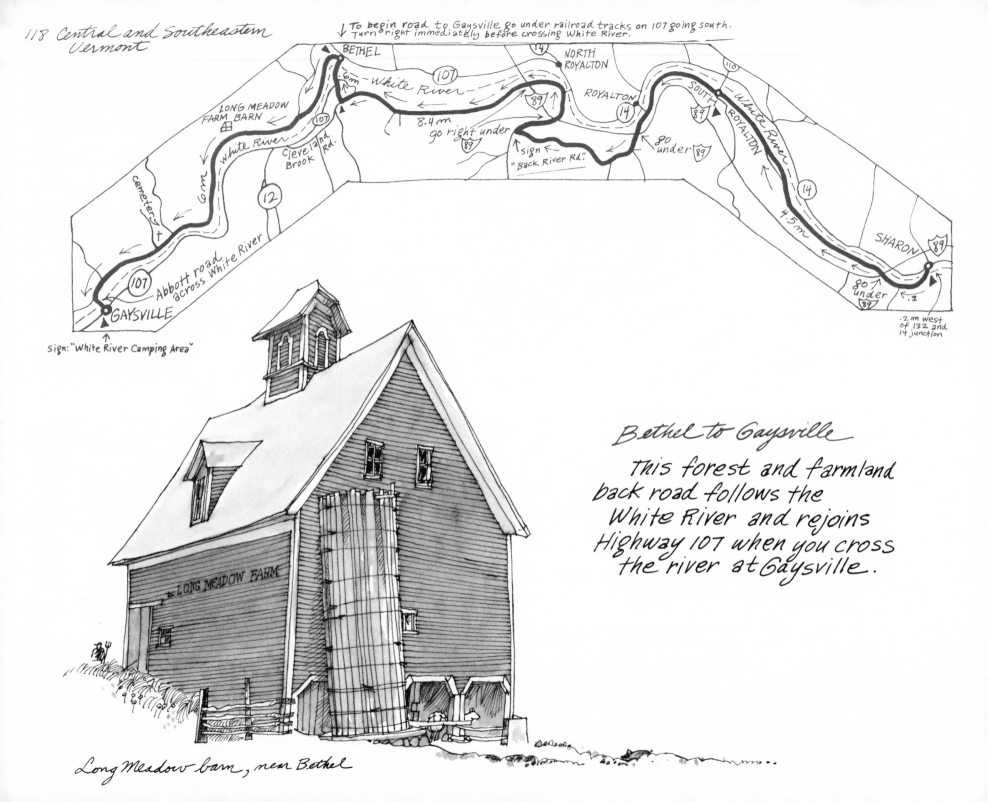

To begin road to Gaysville go under railroad tracks on 107 going south. Turn right immediately before crossing White River.

BETHEL

NORTH ROYALTON

107 White River

.6m

LONG MEADOW FARM BARN

White River

.6m

Cleveland Brook Rd.

cemetery

†

12

107

Abbott road across White River

GAYSVILLE

107

Sign: "White River Camping Area"

8.4m go right under 89

sign "Back River Rd."

ROYALTON

14

89

.80 under 89

SOUTH ROYALTON

89

White River

14

4.5m

SHARON

89

.80 under 89

.2

.2m west of 132 and 14 junction

Bethel to Gaysville

This forest and farmland back road follows the White River and rejoins Highway 107 when you cross the river at Gaysville.

LONG MEADOW FARM

Long Meadow barn, near Bethel

Millpond at Quechee

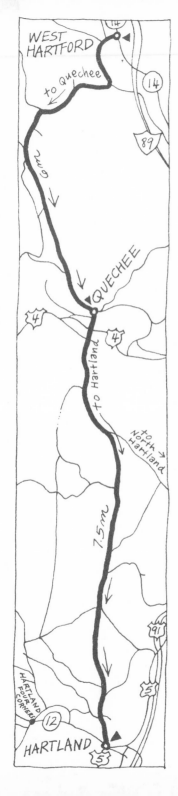

WEST HARTFORD

14

to Quechee

14

89

9.6 m

QUECHEE

4

4

to Hartland

to North Hartland

7.5 m

91

5

HARTLAND FOUR CORNERS

12

HARTLAND

5

← From QUECHEE cross river at covered bridge up Waterman Hill. Cross Highway 4 on Quechee-Hartland Road. Quechee-Hartland Road ends at junction of Highways 5 and 12.

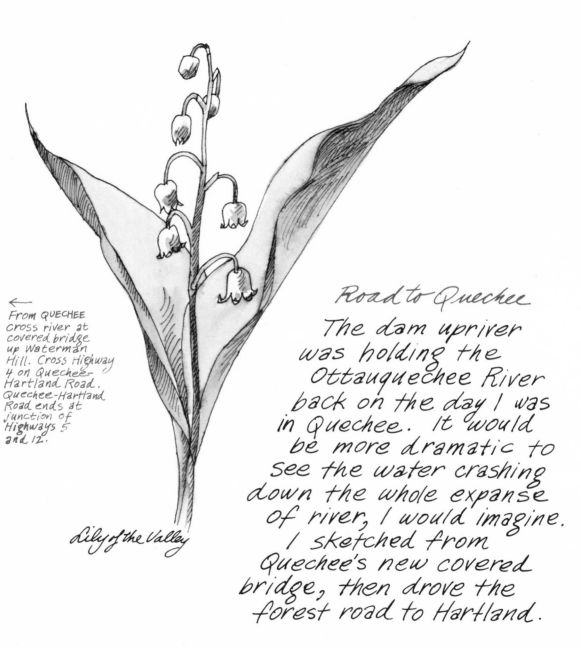

Lily of the Valley

Road to Quechee

The dam upriver was holding the Ottauquechee River back on the day I was in Quechee. It would be more dramatic to see the water crashing down the whole expanse of river, I would imagine. I sketched from Quechee's new covered bridge, then drove the forest road to Hartland.

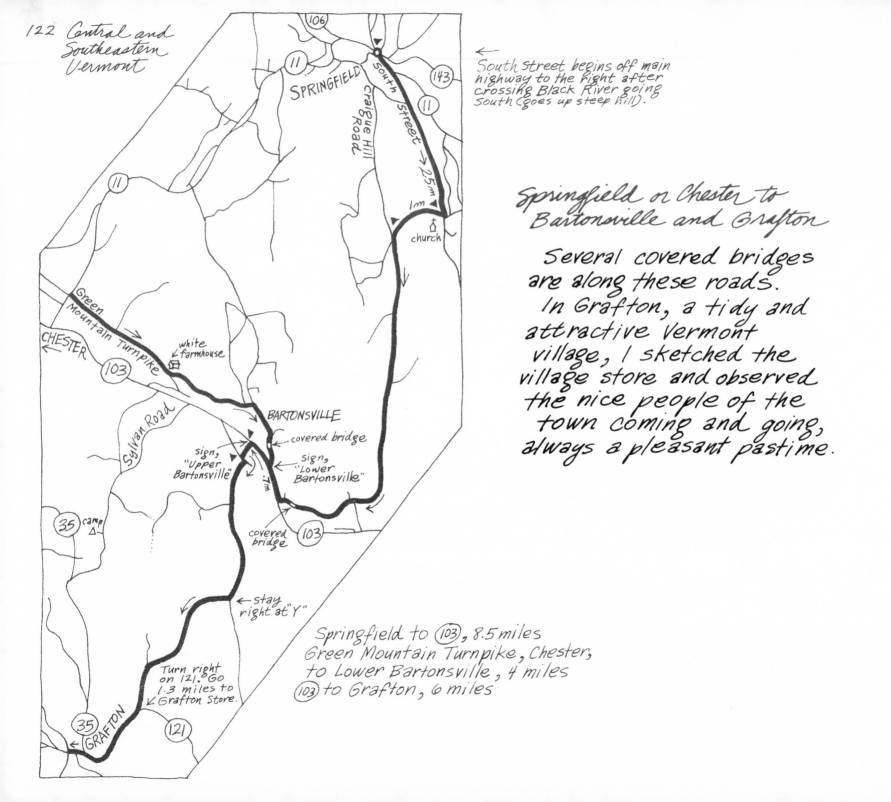

106

11

SPRINGFIELD

143

11

South Street

Craigue Hill Road

2.5m

1m

church

South street begins off main highway to the right after crossing Black River going South (goes up steep hill).

11

11

Green Mountain Turnpike

CHESTER

103

white farmhouse

Sylvan Road

BARTONSVILLE

covered bridge

sign, "Upper Bartonsville"

sign, "Lower Bartonsville"

.7m

covered bridge

103

35

camp △

← stay right at "Y"

Turn right on 121. Go 1.3 miles to Grafton Store.

35

GRAFTON

121

Springfield or Chester to Bartonsville and Grafton

Several covered bridges are along these roads.
In Grafton, a tidy and attractive Vermont village, I sketched the village store and observed the nice people of the town coming and going, always a pleasant pastime.

Springfield to (103), 8.5 miles
Green Mountain Turnpike, Chester, to Lower Bartonsville, 4 miles
(103) to Grafton, 6 miles

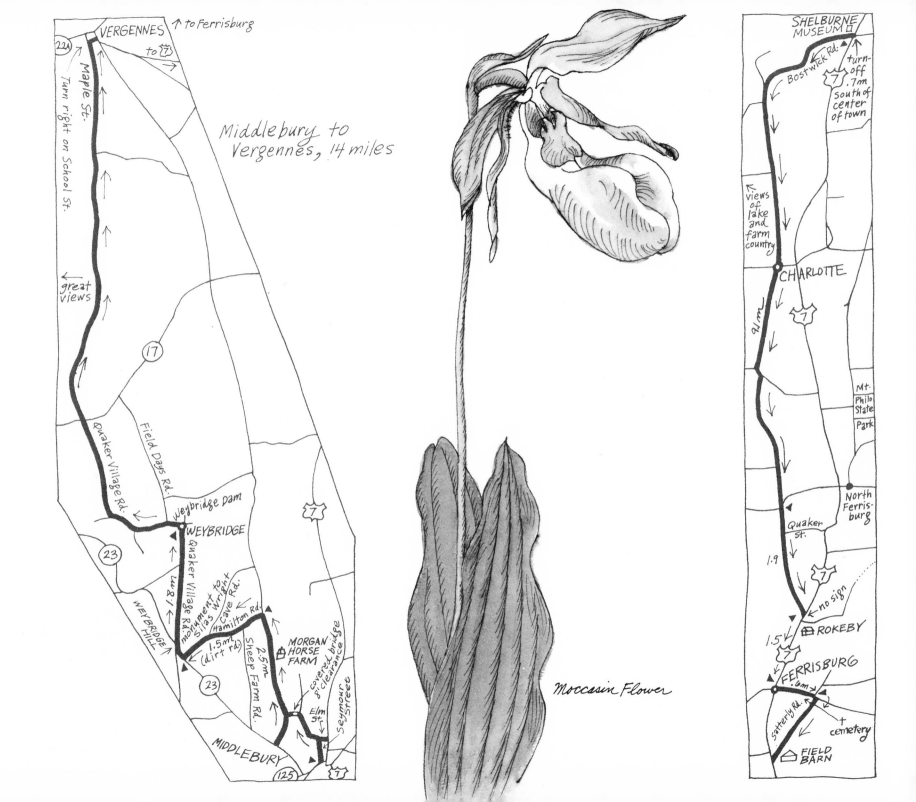

Left map:

↑ to Ferrisburg

VERGENNES

22A

to 7

Maple St.

Turn right on School St.

Middlebury to
Vergennes, 14 miles

← great views

17

Field Days Rd.

Quaker Village Rd.

7

Weybridge Dam

WEYBRIDGE

23

Quaker Village Rd.

monument to Silas Wright

Cave Rd.

Hamilton Rd.

1.8 m.

WEYBRIDGE HILL

1.5 m. (dirt rd.)

Sheep Farm Rd.

2.5 m.

MORGAN HORSE FARM

covered bridge 8' clearance

23

Elm St.

Seymour Street

MIDDLEBURY

125

7

Center illustration:

Moccasin Flower

Right map:

SHELBURNE MUSEUM

Bostwick Rd.

turn-off .7m. south of center of town

7

← views of lake and farm country

9 m.

CHARLOTTE

7

Mt. Philo State Park

Quaker St.

North Ferrisburg

1.9

7

← no sign

1.5

ROKEBY

7

FERRISBURG

.6m. →

Satterly Rd. R.

† cemetery

FIELD BARN

Middlebury to Vergennes

For great distances you can see eye-pleasing views of gently rolling hills, prosperous looking farms and farmland. South of the village of Weybridge is the Morgan Horse Farm where America's first breed of horse, the Morgan, is bred and raised by the University of Vermont.

The horse, Justin Morgan, was born in 1789, and so distinctive was he, sired by an English thoroughbred and a mare of Arabian extraction it is believed, that his line has been carefully bred to this day.

Morgan Horse Farm, Weybridge

Rokeby, Ferrisburg

Rokeby to Charlotte and Shelburne

North of Ferrisburg is Rokeby, the ancestral home of Rowland E. Robinson, Vermont's 19th-century artist, illustrator, writer and folklorist. His home, still completely furnished with the Robinson furniture and effects, is open to visitors during the summer months. Rowland's daughter, Rachael, had sketched her father in the 1890s, so using her original drawing I recreated him for you, sitting beside his kitchen fireplace almost 90 years ago.

Ferrisburg to Buckwheat Street

The Robinson family is buried at the cemetery near Buckwheat Street. Karl Field's eleven-sided barn designed in 1911 is also located on this old country road, once a main road.

Polygonal barn, Ferrisburg

Lake Champlain
Back Road

Boat rigs like this one
are a necessity for
raising and lowering
boats into the
lake. They are on
wheels and can
be pulled
ashore before
winter's
freeze.
Along
this back
road, at
Miltonboro's
shady cemetery,
graves hold the
remains of people
who lived in the
1700s.

Boat rig,
Lake Champlain

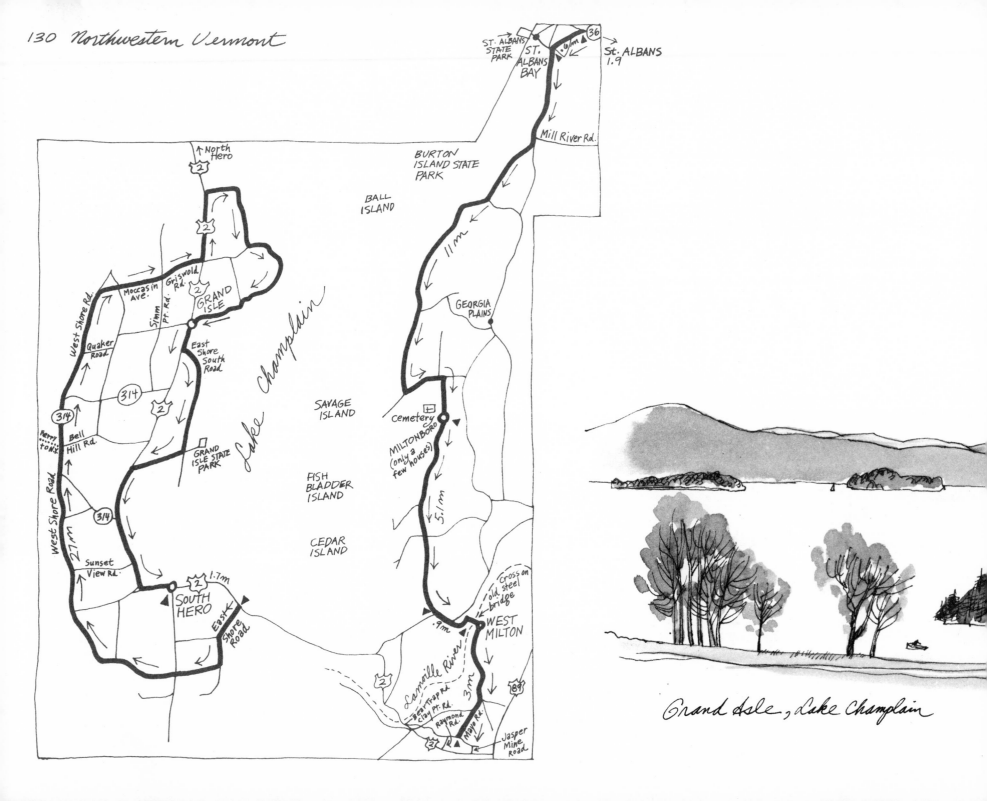

↑North Hero

2

ST. ALBANS STATE PARK

ST. ALBANS BAY

.6m

36

St. ALBANS 1.9

Mill River Rd.

BURTON ISLAND STATE PARK

BALL ISLAND

Moccasin Ave.

West Shore Rd.

Griswold Rd.

2

GRAND ISLE

Simm Pt. Rd.

Quaker Road

East Shore South Road

11m

GEORGIA PLAINS

Lake Champlain

314

2

SAVAGE ISLAND

Cemetery

MILTONBORO (only a few houses)

Ferry to N.Y.

Bell Hill Rd.

GRAND ISLE STATE PARK

FISH BLADDER ISLAND

5.1m

West Shore Road

27m

314

CEDAR ISLAND

Sunset View Rd.

2 1.7m

SOUTH HERO

East Shore Road

cross on old steel bridge

WEST MILTON

.9m

Lamoille River

Beartrap Rd.

Clay Pt. Rd.

Raymond Rd.

Mayo Rd.

3m

89

2

Jasper Mine Road

Grand Isle, Lake Champlain

Grand Isle and South Hero

Back roads pass through rolling countryside, farmed
 by Americans since the Revolution when war heroes
 received land grants. In 1783 this area joined the
"Free and Independent Republic of Vermont."

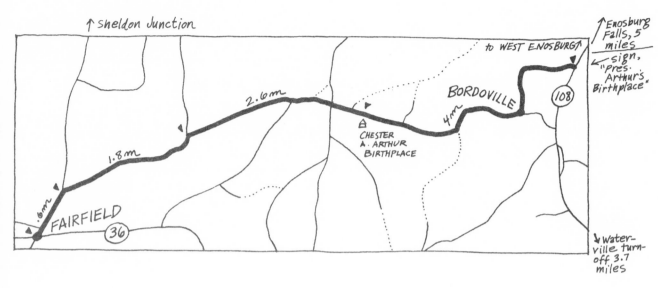

Fairfield to Bordoville

There are long views of attractive farming land along this country road. Near Bordoville is the birthplace of our 21st United States president, Chester A. Arthur.

On the road, Fairfield to Bordoville

From Johnson the road begins immediately after crossing the Lamoille River 3/10 mile from town.

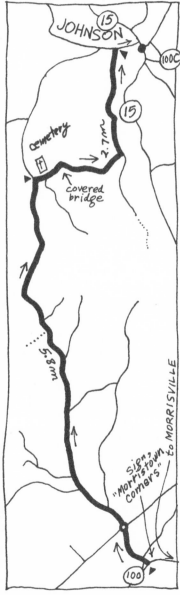

JOHNSON

15

100C

15

Cemetery

2.7m

covered bridge

5.8m

Sign, "Morristown Corners" to MORRISVILLE

to MORRISVILLE

100

108

↑ 3.7 miles to Chester Arthur birthplace turnoff

108

1.7m

.5m

← to Bakersfield

6.5m

covered bridge

3m

BELVIDERE CENTER

109

↑ covered bridge

BELVIDERE JUNCTION

3.5m

← covered bridge

← covered bridge

109

covered bridge →

WATERVILLE

109

Lamoille River

5.5m

1.7 miles from JOHNSON

15

Morrisville to Johnson

Arriving at Johnson from Morrisville was unique; the road passed through a working lumber mill. I got permission to sketch the "log debarker" and emerged from the experience with ears ringing and bark chips down my neck.

The logs on the right are having their bark removed by the churning saw blade. Those on the left are on their way to be sawed into planks.

The lumber company is no longer in operation, yet the beauty of this back road trip remains.

Road begins out of Johnson just west of bridge crossing Lamoille River. It is marked by a sign saying, "The Long Trail." Upon reaching 109 jog left almost 4/10 mile and turn right on dirt road.

Log debarker, Manchester Lumber Company,
Johnson

Johnson to Waterville

It is a pleasant drive from Johnson to Waterville along the meandering Lamoille River.

The bandstand in Waterville used to bulge with 22 musicians on concert nights, but that was decades ago. The Town Hall was once a church, then a library. The clock tower was added to get sufficient height for its pendulum.

WATERVILLE
SETTLED BY
TIMOTHY BROWN
AND WIFE
MEREDITH WARD BROWN
1779

Town Hall, Waterville

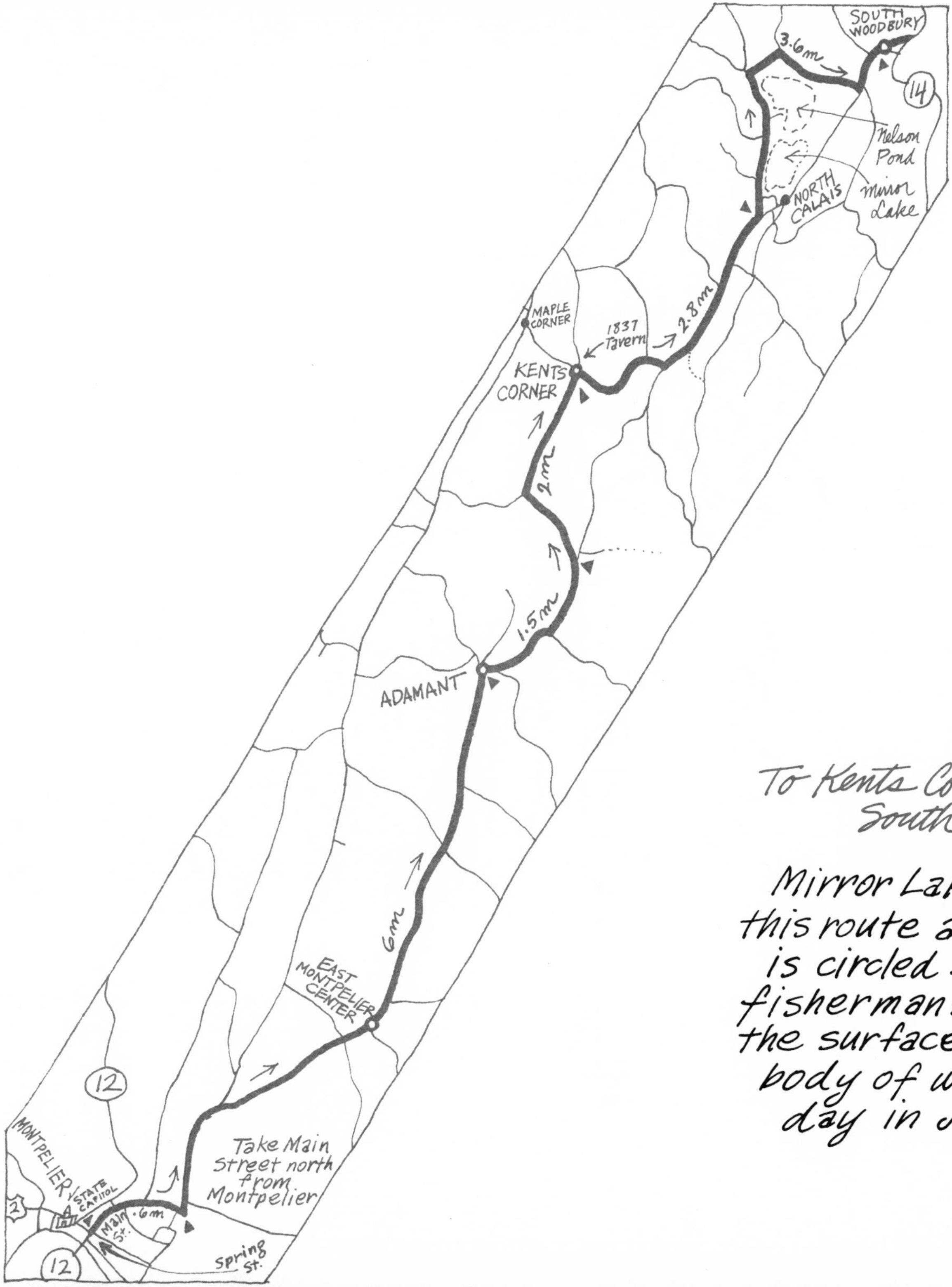

SOUTH
WOODBURY

3.6m

14

Nelson
Pond

Mirror
Lake

NORTH
CALAIS

2.8m

MAPLE
CORNER

1837
Tavern

KENTS
CORNER

2m

1.5m

ADAMANT

6m

EAST
MONTPELIER
CENTER

12

MONTPELIER

STATE
CAPITOL

2

Main .6m
St.

12

spring
St.

Take Main
Street north
from
Montpelier

To Kents Corner and
South Woodbury

Mirror Lake is passed on
this route and Nelson Pond
is circled. Only one
fisherman's boat broke
the surface of this placid
body of water on that
day in June.

Nelson Pond, Calais

John George's "Idle Hours Farm" on the Mackville Road offers very few idle hours for this farmer. Taking care of his beloved cows takes all of his time. I sketched and he spoke personally to each cow as he placed the milkers or removed them.

The one-day-old calf doing the licking in the picture never seemed to tire of this occupation. Even the kitten got lapped.

John George's "Idle Hours Farm", near Hardwick

Marway Farm near Hardwick

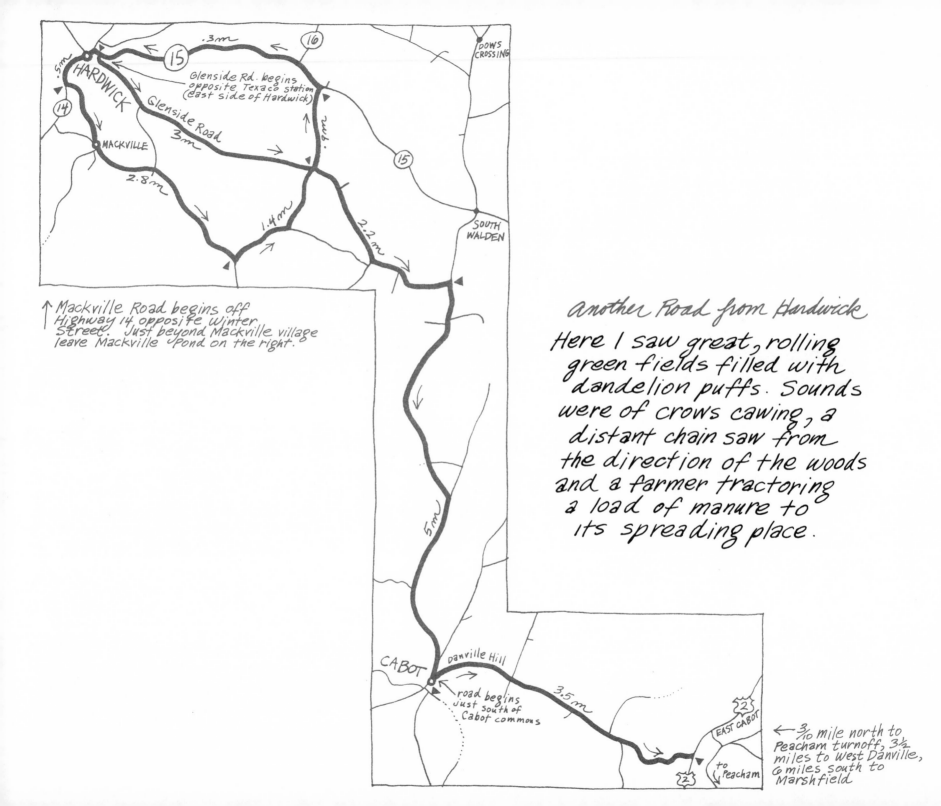

.3m

15

16

5m

HARDWICK

14

Glenside Rd. begins
opposite Texaco station
(east side of Hardwick)

Glenside Road

3m

MACKVILLE

2.8m

1.4m

.9m

2.2m

15

DOWS
CROSSING

SOUTH
WALDEN

↑ Mackville Road begins off
Highway 14 opposite Winter
Street. Just beyond Mackville village
leave Mackville Pond on the right.

5m

another Road from Hardwick

Here I saw great, rolling
green fields filled with
dandelion puffs. Sounds
were of crows cawing, a
distant chain saw from
the direction of the woods
and a farmer tractoring
a load of manure to
its spreading place.

CABOT

Danville Hill

road begins
just south of
Cabot commons

3.5 m

2

EAST CABOT

to
Peacham

2

← 3/10 mile north to
Peacham turnoff, 3½
miles to West Danville,
6 miles south to
Marshfield

Peacham and Danville Roads

Church bells chimed a melody at halfpast the hour
out over quiet Peacham village.
From Peacham, just above South Danville,
there is a neat, short covered bridge over
rushing Joe's Brook.

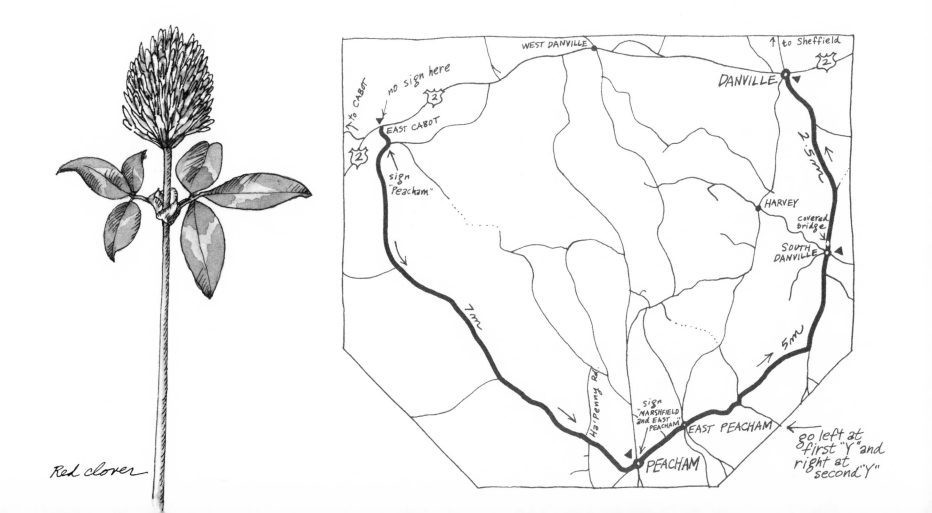

Red clover

Peacham

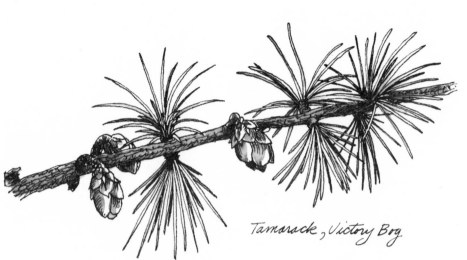

Tamarack, Victory Bog

North Concord to Sheffield to Danville

Here is a back road along the Moose River through the primitive flat landscape of Victory Bog, an area of little population. Leaving the river and going west toward Burke Hollow, the land becomes hilly again and farms reappear.

Front porch wash, West Burke

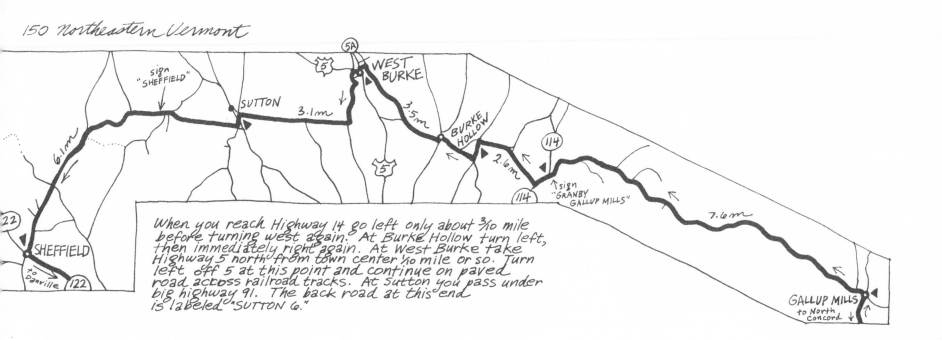

When you reach Highway 14 go left only about 3/10 mile before turning west again. At Burke Hollow turn left, then immediately right again. At West Burke take Highway 5 north from town center 1/10 mile or so. Turn left off 5 at this point and continue on paved road across railroad tracks. At Sutton you pass under big highway 91. The back road at this end is labeled "SUTTON 6."

Robin Plantain

From West Burke to Sutton there is rolling farmland and some thick forest and then a picturesque view approaching Sheffield.

The postmistress told me that the town was "just a small farming community of people who cooperate with one another."

Sheffield

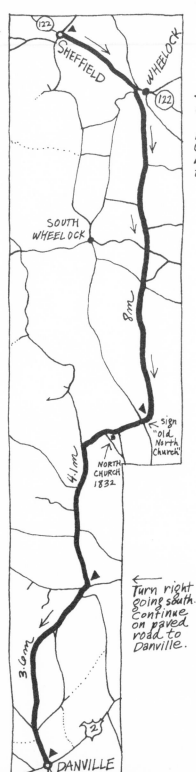

122

SHEFFIELD

WHEELOCK

122

← Turn right (south) just north of Wheelock off Highway 122. Cross bridge and begin the back road to Danville.

SOUTH WHEELOCK

8m

← Sign "Old North Church"

NORTH CHURCH 1832

4.1m

← Turn right going south. Continue on paved road to Danville.

3.6m

2

DANVILLE

wild cherry

I reached Danville as the postmaster was lowering the flag at the end of day. Since my drawing was made, the post office has moved to its own building on the other side of the common.

POST OFFICE
DANVILLE

Danville

New Hampshire

Northern New Hampshire is an area of massive mountains. There are few back roads branching off into those precipitous chasms. Adjacent to the mountains however, as in Vermont, back roads are delightful to travel and you may experience joy in the beauty of the landscape.

Blue Flag

LISBON
SUGAR HILL
BATH
EASTON
WENTWORTH
ELLSWORTH
CONWAY
WEST CAMPTON
EAST MADISON
EFFINGHAM FALLS
WEST RUMNEY
RUMNEY
CHEEVER
TUFTONBORO
OSSIPEE
GROTON
HEBRON
CENTER TUFTONBORO
BELMONT
GILMANTON IRONWORKS
LOWER GILMANTON
SHAKER VILLAGE
CENTER BARNSTEAD
EAST CONCORD

New Hampshire

Back Road to Lisbon

The back road to Lisbon offers a long view of the town across the Ammonoosuc River. Just before crossing the bridge there's a lawn and benches, a place to sketch and to listen to the roar of the falls. The town was once known as Concord, then Chiswick, followed by Gunthwaite; however, in 1824 it became Lisbon after the great Portuguese city. Saying "Liz-bon" slowly sounds good and vibrates the tongue and brain, I discovered.

Ammonoosuc River at Lisbon

Klay Knoll Farm, Bath

The Road to Bath

I tried to include as much as I could of 600-acre Klay Knoll Farm. Farmer Lester Presby is pictured three times, first emerging on the right as he started his tractor, later on climbing the road on the left to spread some manure, then finally in the foreground "teddering" (turning the hay over to dry).

Enter Bath over the long covered bridge and see its fine brick buildings including the old country store.

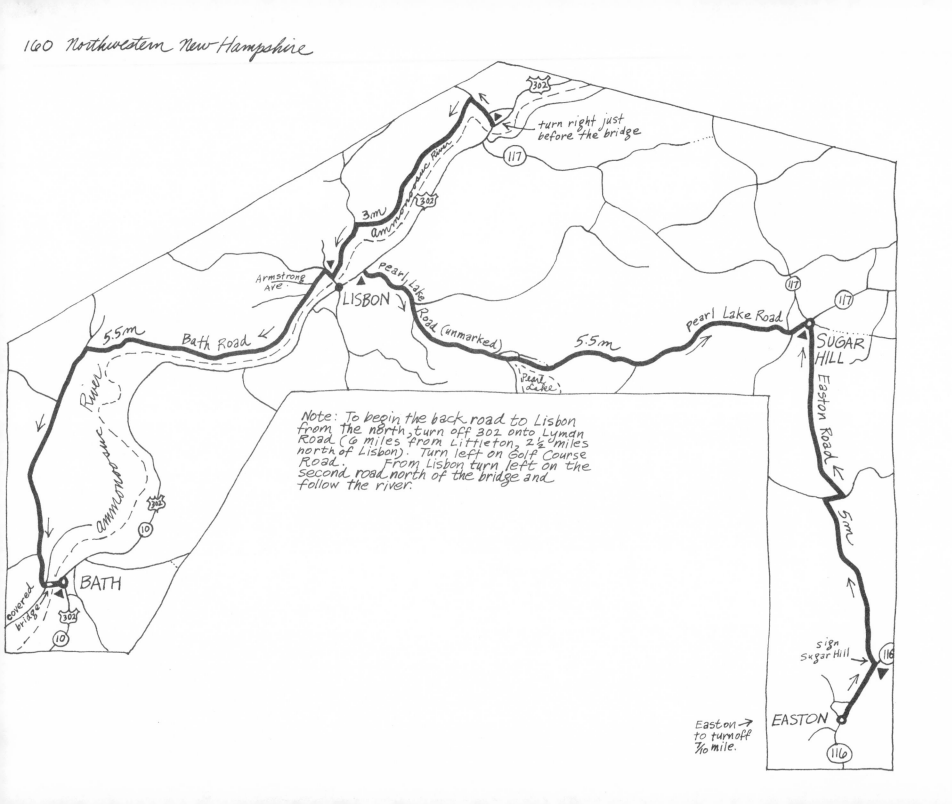

302

turn right just
before the bridge

117

3m

Ammonoosuc River

302

Armstrong
Ave.

Pearl Lake
Road (unmarked)

LISBON

5.5m

Bath Road

5.5m

Pearl Lake Road

117

117

Pearl
Lake

SUGAR
HILL

Ammonoosuc
River

Easton Road

302

10

Note: To begin the back road to Lisbon
from the north, turn off 302 onto Lyman
Road (6 miles from Littleton, 2½ miles
north of Lisbon). Turn left on Golf Course
Road. From Lisbon turn left on the
second road north of the bridge and
follow the river.

5m

covered
bridge

BATH

302

10

sign
Sugar Hill

116

Easton →
to turnoff
7/10 mile.

EASTON

116

Lester Presby,
Klay Knoll Farm, Bath

Roads to Sugar Hill

These marvelous picture-inspiring roads begin in Lisbon and Easton. In Sugar Hill people remember the Sweetpea Farm when it actually sold sweetpeas to the many large summer hotels that once flourished in this area. Today the farm is a fine private home restored by the Jessemans. The left side was built in 1830, the right in 1887, the vintage car in 1929, I think.

Sweet Pea Farm, Sugar Hill

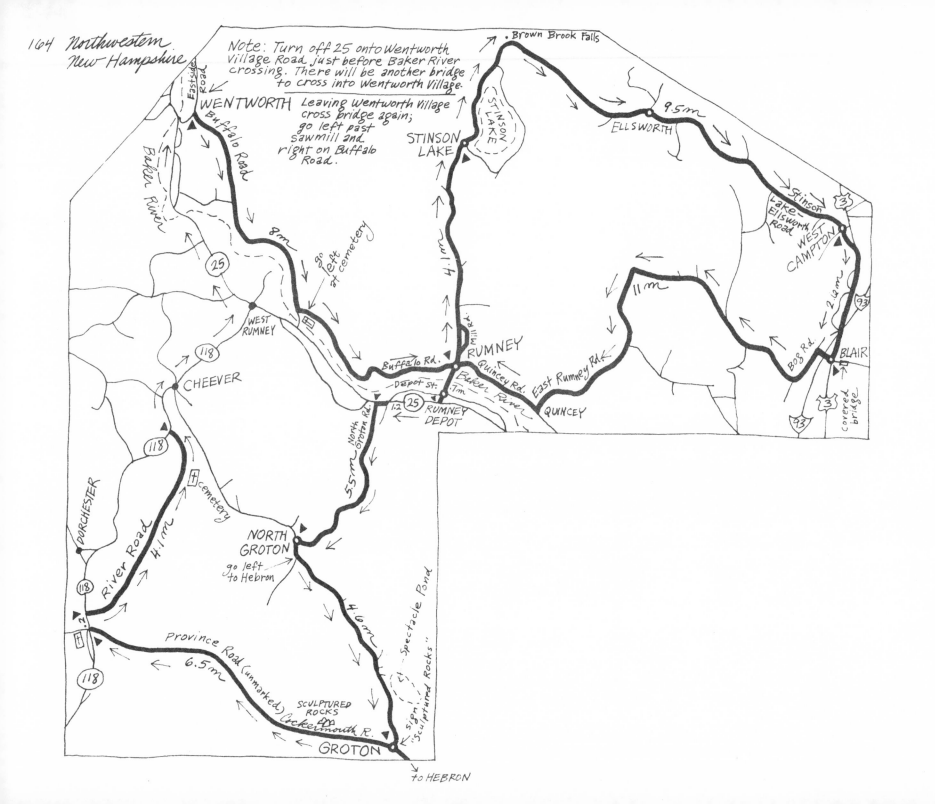

Note: Turn off 25 onto Wentworth Village Road just before Baker River crossing. There will be another bridge to cross into Wentworth Village.

Leaving Wentworth Village cross bridge again; go left past sawmill and right on Buffalo Road.

Brown Brook Falls

STINSON LAKE

STINSON LAKE

9.5m

ELLSWORTH

Stinson Lake-Ellsworth Road

WEST CAMPTON

2.4m

3

93

BLAIR

covered bridge

3

93

WENTWORTH

Eastside Road

Buffalo Road

Baker River

25

8m

go left at cemetery

WEST RUMNEY

4.1m

RUMNEY

Buffalo Rd.

Quincey Rd.

East Rumney Rd.

11m

Bog Rd.

118

CHEEVER

Depot St.

Baker River

.7m

25

1.2

RUMNEY DEPOT

QUINCEY

5.5m North Groton Rd.

DORCHESTER

118

River Road

4.1m

cemetery

118

NORTH GROTON

go left to Hebron

4.6m

Spectacle Pond

sign "Sculptured Rocks"

118

Province Road (unmarked)

6.5m

SCULPTURED ROCKS

Cockermouth R.

GROTON

to HEBRON

Road Along the Cockermouth River

Past the picturesque village of Hebron and out of Groton is the geological masterpiece, "Sculptured Rocks", shaped through time by rushing, charging water. From here the road narrows and becomes more primitive. To me it was like proceeding through a hole in the forest, the beauty of the woods closer about me than on any other drive. This was the most adventurous of my back roads trips through New England.

Sculptured Rocks near Groton

Lupine

Wentworth to Rumney

The post office on the common
in Wentworth has church notices
in the window including a plea
for the organ fund. There was
also the following, "Piano
Recitals by the pupils of
Marcella Hoffman, Russell
School, Rumney." Several cows
grazed in the meadow behind
the post office as I read
each and every item.

Roads to Rumney

Along River Road, as in many places in New England, rock walls indicating old farm fields and boundaries vanish from view as brush and trees grow back.

In Rumney I sketched the former home of the founder of Christian Science, Mary Baker Eddy.

There are notable mountain views on the road past Stinson Lake to West Campton.

From Rumney, again, you climb toward North Groton with a churning river at your side.

Mary Baker Eddy house, Rumney

Smooth
Yellow Violet

Bunchberry

Back Roads Wildflowers
Engage the Eye
    All through this book are
my drawings of New England
wildflowers. They were fun
for this back road traveler
 to discover and catalog.
I would wish that you, too,
 will notice the wildflowers
and appreciate their
   intricate and flawless
   beauty.

False Solomon's Seal

Hobblebush

Bladder Campion

The Road Past Shaker Village

It was only a few years ago that the Paul Revere bell was re-identified in the belfry of the old Dwelling House at Shaker Village. This building was chapel and dining hall for the Shaker religious sect in 1825. The road past Shaker Village from Concord ends among the handsome white homes of Belmont town.

Note: To begin road going north on 93, take exit 16. Go left on 132 and 3B, then right in 3/10 mile on Shaker Road. Cross Hoit Road in about 3 3/10 miles. Shaker Road becomes dirt at this point. Starting from Belmont you would go south on Main Street.

The Dwelling House,
Shaker Village

Road to Gilmanton Ironworks

Cemeteries in New England
are fascinating sculptural
entities. And, perhaps
nowhere else in these United
States are there so many of
them. The road from Center
Barnstead to the hillside
village of Gilmanton Ironworks
and Crystal Lake passes
this little cemetery with the
gazebo in the center.

Orange Hawkweed

Caraway.

Gilmanton Ironworks cemetery

Road to Center Barnstead

The church at Center Barnstead has an old-fashioned interior with a great, low, hanging chandelier. Pews face the front door, to the dismay of those who find themselves late for service and must face the entire congregation while proceeding to their seats.

The Soldier and Sailor Memorial in front of the church is in memory of those who died in the wars of 1776-83, 1812-14, 1846-48, 1861-65 and 1917-19. Flags flying from many a gravesite and memorial are placed by the American Legion.

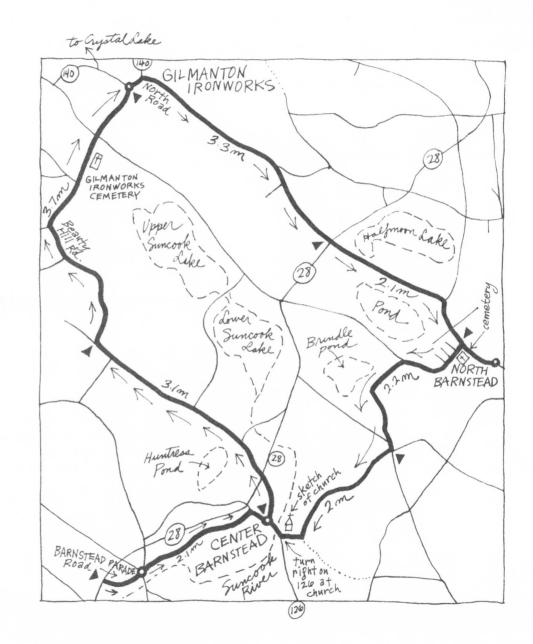

Center Barnstead

Two Roads to Ossipee

From Center Tuftonboro or farther east from North Wakefield good country roads lead to Ossipee.

The Walter White house in Ossipee has many additions. Originally the main house was a small "Cape-Codder," vintage 1850. It was then raised up one story and the barn to the left added. The elevated porch provided the occupants a place to sit and watch the carriages go by. The addition on the right was once a millinery shop, then a restaurant, and now is part of the main house. The latest addition, in 1952, is the garage on the left with an elephant weatherrane celebrating Eisenhower's election to the presidency.

A house in Ossipee

E. MADISON

PORTER ME

FREEDOM

SOUTH
EATON
SETTLED
1766

Sign at South Eaton

Backroad through Effingham Falls
to East Madison

The Davis barn near Effingham
Falls sits solidly on great granite
blocks, cut and fitted neatly to form
a permanent base for the heavily
timbered barn. Some pillars inside
on the ground floor are also
granite. Part of the original
granite corral is on the other
side of the barn.

The Davis Farm near Effingham

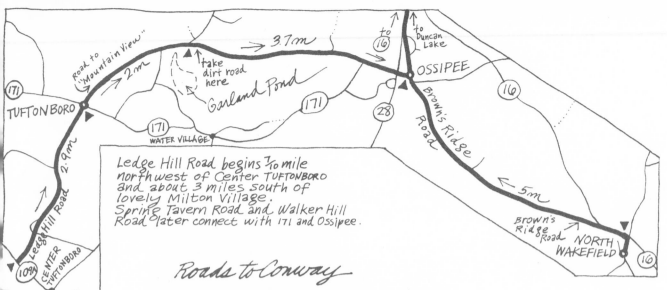

to Duncan Lake

Ledge Hill Road begins 7/10 mile northwest of Center TUFTONBORO and about 3 miles south of lovely Milton Village.
Spring Tavern Road and Walker Hill Road later connect with 171 and Ossipee.

Roads to Conway

Eaton Center to Center Conway around Conway Lake is a fine forest drive. West of Conway another forest drive begins off Highway 112 near Lower Falls Camp, White Mountain National Forest, where the covered bridge crosses Swift River.

While I drew the bridge's profile, hikers with packs, boys on bicycles carrying fishing rods, and numerous auto campers emerged. Suddenly, a man appeared wheeling a baby in a stroller, and this I recorded for you.

A young man who had been climbing the bridge's timbers to impress his girl friend, came over to borrow a needle to take out a splinter. When he had successfully done so, he agreed to pose and so he, too, I sketched, sitting in the window of the covered bridge.

Horse Leg Hill Road

EAST MADISON   SOUTH EATON

153   3.4m

go right toward Freedom

153   2.4m

EFFINGHAM FALLS   25 153

25   Green Mt. Rd.   DAVIS FARM

.8m

cross small bridge, go left at "T"

from 16 take road between Duncan Lake Rest and Twombly's Golden Dairy Treat - where lone chimney stands, turn right

16   Duncan Lake

to Ossipee

take Elm Street to right in 3/10 mile.

16

Bridge over the Swift River, near Conway

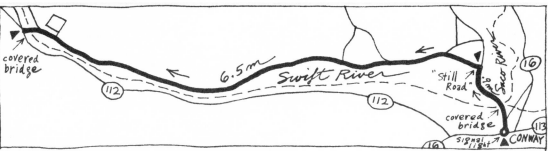

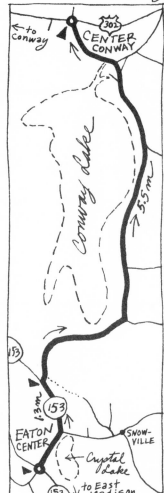

Take Mill Street (Conway Lake) from this end going south

From Conway go north on West Side Road. You will see the old covered bridge bypassed on the right. Turn west on Still Road and continue on, passing Dugway Picnic Area on the left and finally reaching the covered bridge still in use.

Dwarf Cinquefoil

meadow Rue

Maine

The large state of Maine gives one
the feeling of being completely
    engulfed by forests. After
traveling the interior back
    roads through hundreds of
miles of beautiful woods and
    lakes I felt a longing to see
the coast and the ocean.
    The northern coast of Maine
was my area of exploration.

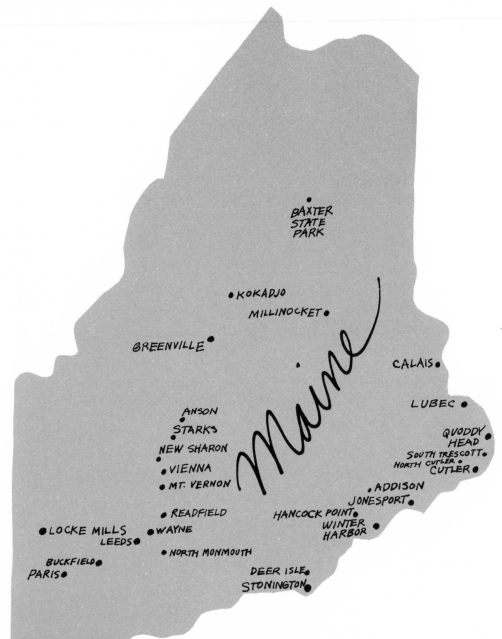

Maine

BAXTER
STATE
PARK

KOKADJO
MILLINOCKET

GREENVILLE

CALAIS

ANSON
STARKS
NEW SHARON
VIENNA
MT. VERNON

LUBEC

QUODDY
HEAD
SOUTH TRESCOTT
NORTH CUTLER
CUTLER

ADDISON
JONESPORT

READFIELD
HANCOCK POINT
WINTER
HARBOR

LOCKE MILLS · WAYNE
LEEDS

BUCKFIELD
PARIS
NORTH MONMOUTH

DEER ISLE
STONINGTON

South Pond to
Pennesseewasee Lake

The road from Locke Mills
hugged South Pond for
several miles. The
pond's surface
was unruffled and
the water appeared
dark and mysterious.
There are three
more ponds along
this road before
one reaches the
big Pennesseewasee.

Road along South Pond near Locke Mills

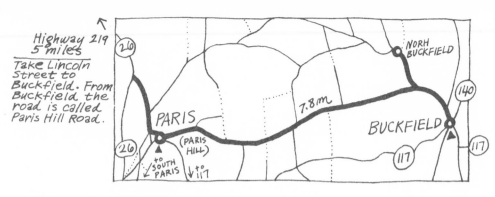

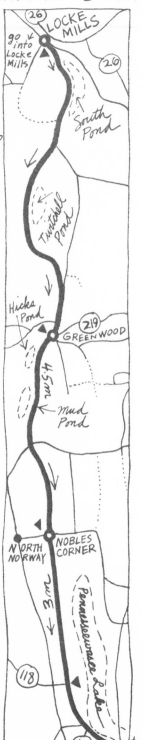

To begin road, turn at sign for Greenwood into Locke Mills village. Take the road to the left of the hill road. Go past South Pond.

Highway 219
5 miles
Take Lincoln Street to Buckfield. From Buckfield the road is called Paris Hill Road.

Road to Paris

The stone jail on the Paris common is built with huge blocks of granite. An X marks the spot on the outside where a stone was successfully removed by an escapee.

The stone was replaced and fastened over the spot to ensure against this happening again. That was a long time ago, for the jail has been the Paris Library since 1900.   Hannibal Hamlin, vice-president to Lincoln, lived in the house just north of the jail, and the view from here toward the White Mountains of New Hampshire is quite dramatic.

Paris, or Paris Hill as it is also called, evokes the atmosphere of another age.

The stone jail, Paris

Paris to Buckfield

On the road to North Buckfield I sketched this mailbox arrangement. The farmer had an old post he thought he'd put to use, he told me, and the wire pulling the chain is meant to keep the mailbox out of the way of the snowplow come winter.

mail rig, Buckfield

Snow flag, Paris

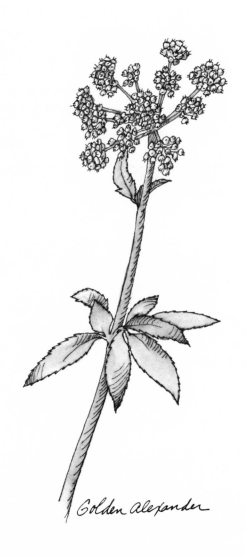

Golden Alexander

North Monmouth and the Androscoggin

This trip meanders along the Androscoggin River to the tiny community of West Leeds, then past Androscoggin Lake and Wilson Pond. At North Monmouth Moncena Burnham had created a water-powered miniature carnival with dolls as participants. At night the display continued with colored lights revolving along with the dolls in gay carnival fashion. When Burnham died, his creation had to be dismantled; however, you can still stand on the little bridge at Main Street North and Wilson Pond Road and allow my drawing to picture it for you.

miniature carnival by water power,
North Monmouth

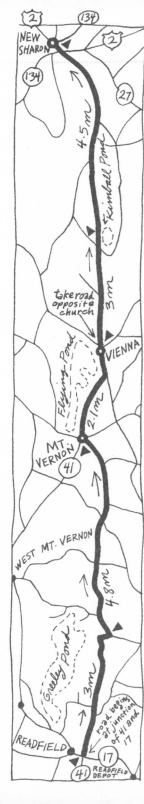

Readfield to
New Sharon

From Readfield
a country road
goes past
farmhouses,
meadows, some
forest, three
cemeteries, rock
walls, and, finally,
down to Mt. Vernon
on Minnehonk Pond.
Carriage builders
once worked here and
there used to be a
gristmill.
   A little farther
north is the neat
village of Vienna
(pronounced "Vy-enna").
   A primitive road past
Kimball Pond goes on to
New Sharon; however you
must ask locally about the
condition of the road.

Mt. Vernon

Detail showing
entry into New
Sharon

Gbl

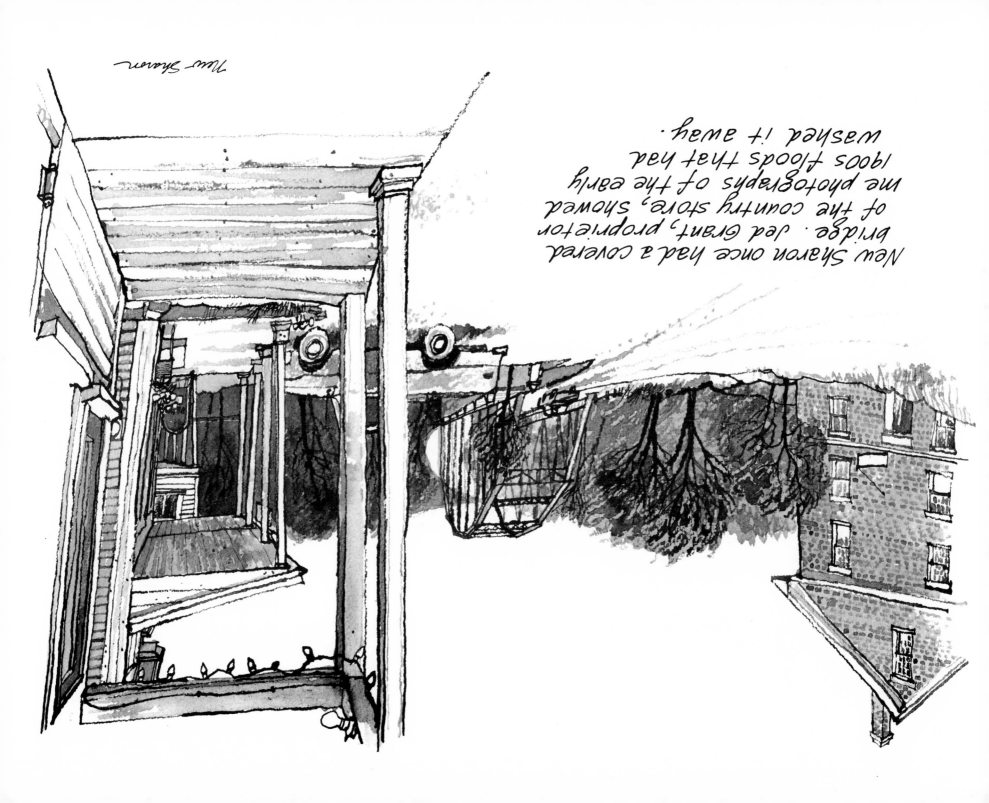

New Sharon once had a covered bridge. Jed Grant, proprietor of the country store, showed me photographs of the early 1900s floods that had washed it away.

New Sharon to Starks

The Frederick Farm is about a mile north of the sleepy town of Starks. Five generations of this family of farmers are buried in the cemetery on the nearby hill. Mr. Frederick told me, "Painting pictures come natural. That I could never do. Milking cows, now, that I can do. Been milking cows for fifty years and that come natural to me!" The Frederick sons are not farmers, so the hard work of carrying on the family farm may end with this older generation.

The covered bridge was replaced in 1910 by the steel one you see in my drawing. In the 50s a new bridge bypassed it. The old one is still used but is closed to lumber trucks and school buses. Ride over it. There is no danger, I'm sure, but with the Sandy River far below there is the feeling that one should really hurry a bit to the safety of the opposite bank.

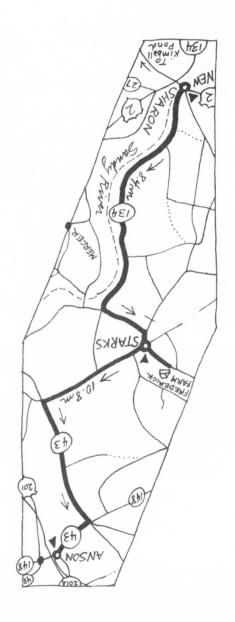

198 Southwestern Maine

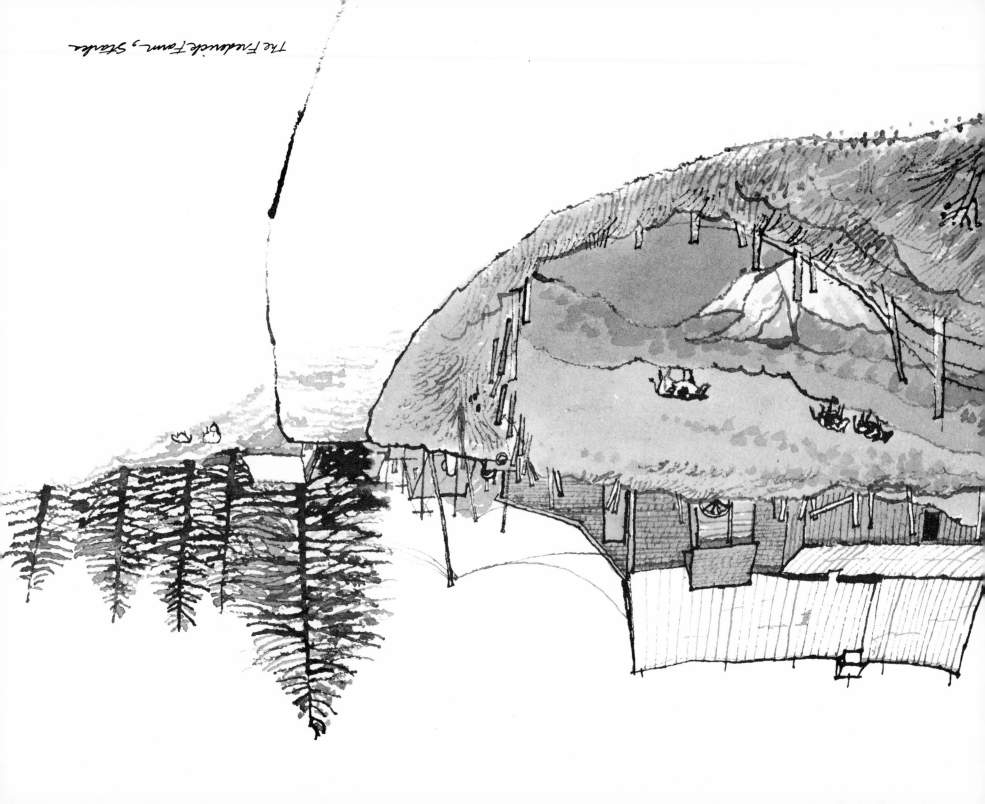

Greenville to Millinocket

This longest back road in the book goes about 70 miles through both public and private lands. Some 15 miles past Lily Bay is a point where you record for private landholders where you are from and what your purpose is. "Riding" was mine.

I sketched Baxter State Park's Mt. Katahdin, the bit of United States territory, it was claimed, that receives the first light of the sun each morning. Percival Baxter, former governor of Maine, purchased and gave this land to Maine, saying "Man is born to die, his works are short-lived, buildings crumble, monuments decay, wealth vanishes, but Katahdin shall remain the mountain of the people of Maine."

Mt. Katahdin

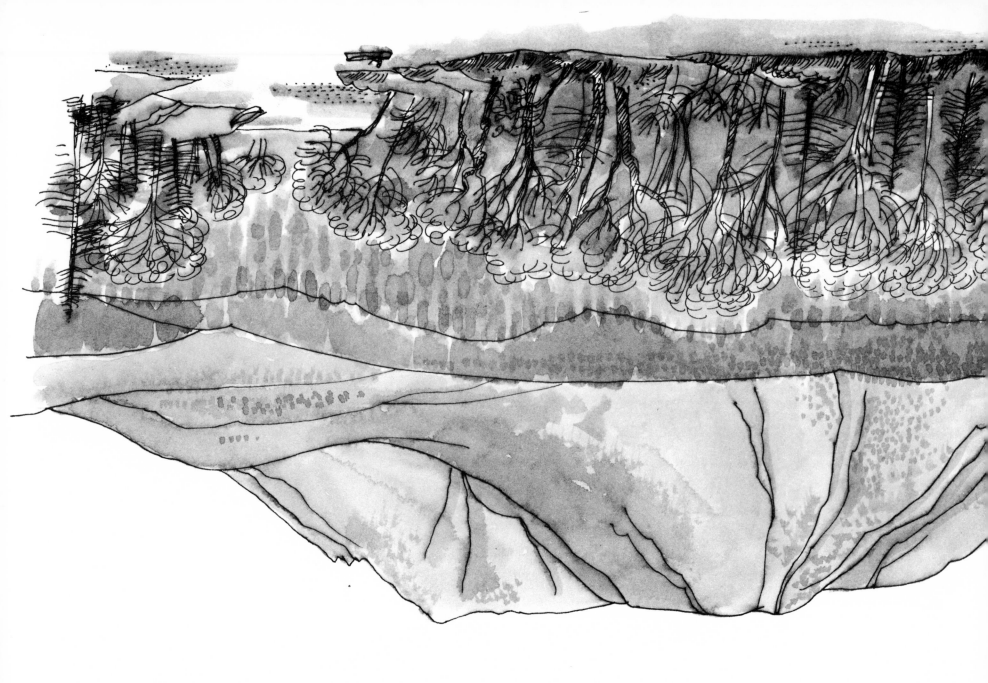

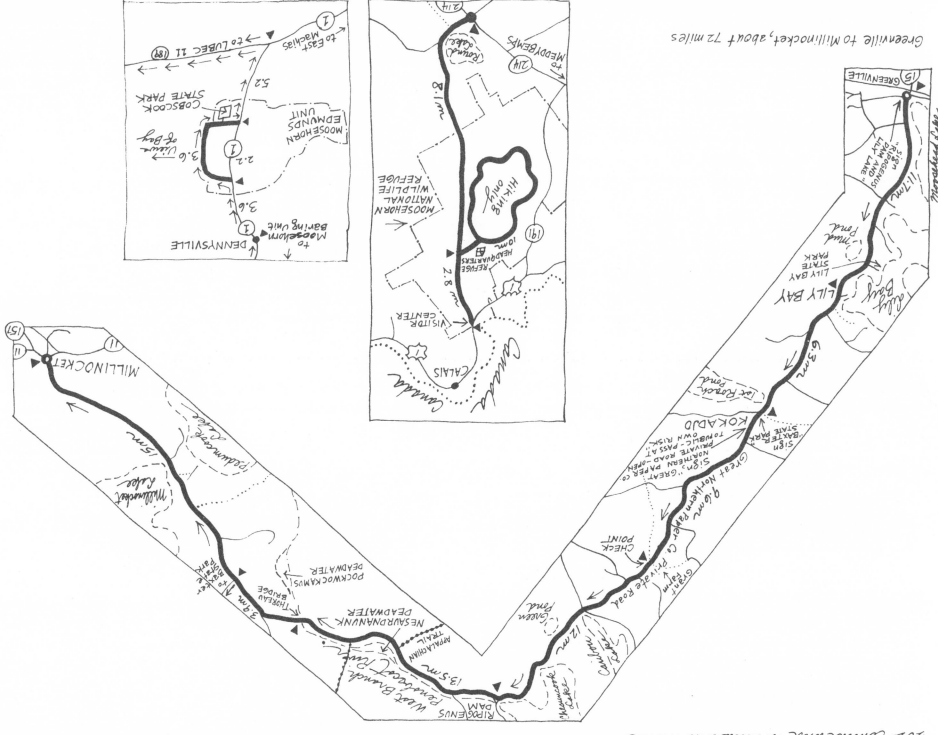

Greenville to Millinocket, about 72 miles

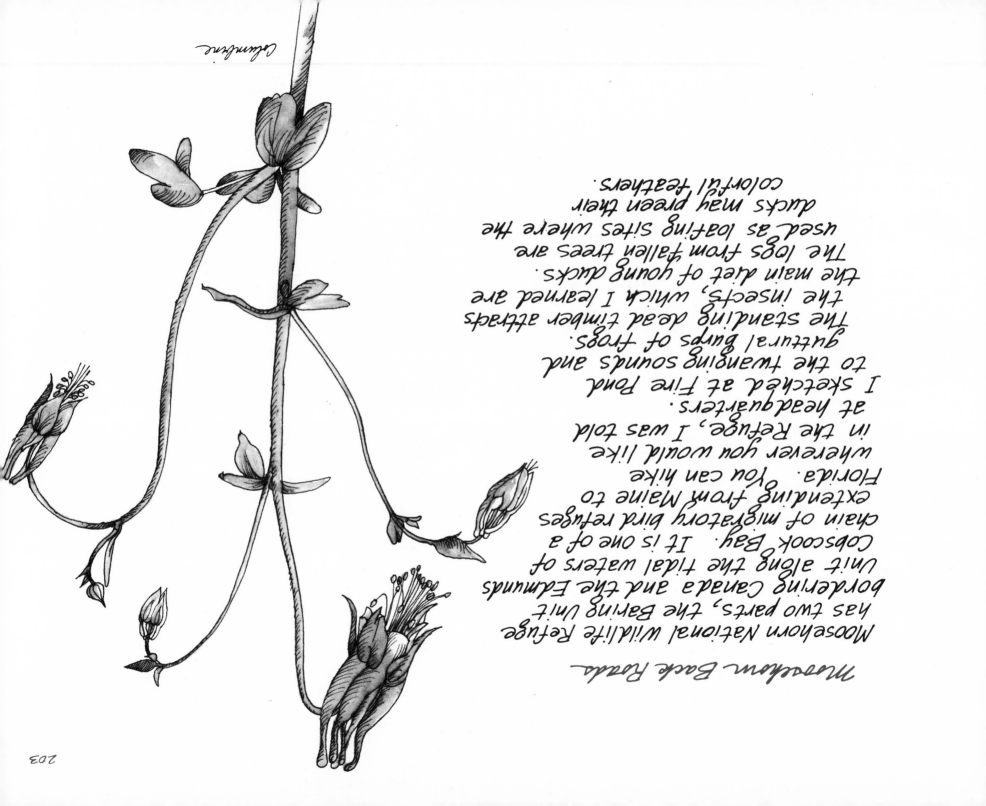

Columbine

Meadow Back Roads

Moosehorn National Wildlife Refuge
has two parts, the Baring Unit
bordering Canada and the Edmunds
Unit along the tidal waters of
Cobscook Bay. It is one of a
chain of migratory bird refuges
extending from Maine to
Florida. You can hike
wherever you would like
in the Refuge, I was told
at headquarters.
    I sketched at Fire Pond
to the twanging sounds and
guttural burps of frogs.
The standing dead timber attracts
the insects, which I learned are
the main diet of young ducks.
The logs from fallen trees are
used as loafing sites where the
ducks may preen their
colorful feathers.

Pine Pond, Moosehorn National Wildlife Refuge

Ox-eye Daisy

From Lubec

Near the Canadian border, on the
ocean, is Lubec. The tide was
out and the fog thick in the
hilly, picturesque, fishing village
as I sketched old Pike's Wharf.
Although International Bridge to
Campobello Island was in the
background it was lost from view.
Franklin Delano Roosevelt would visit
Campobello by taking the boat
from Eastport, but now you can
visit his old summer home by
merely crossing the auto bridge
at Lubec.

Pilot's Wharf, Dublin

2010 Marine Carol

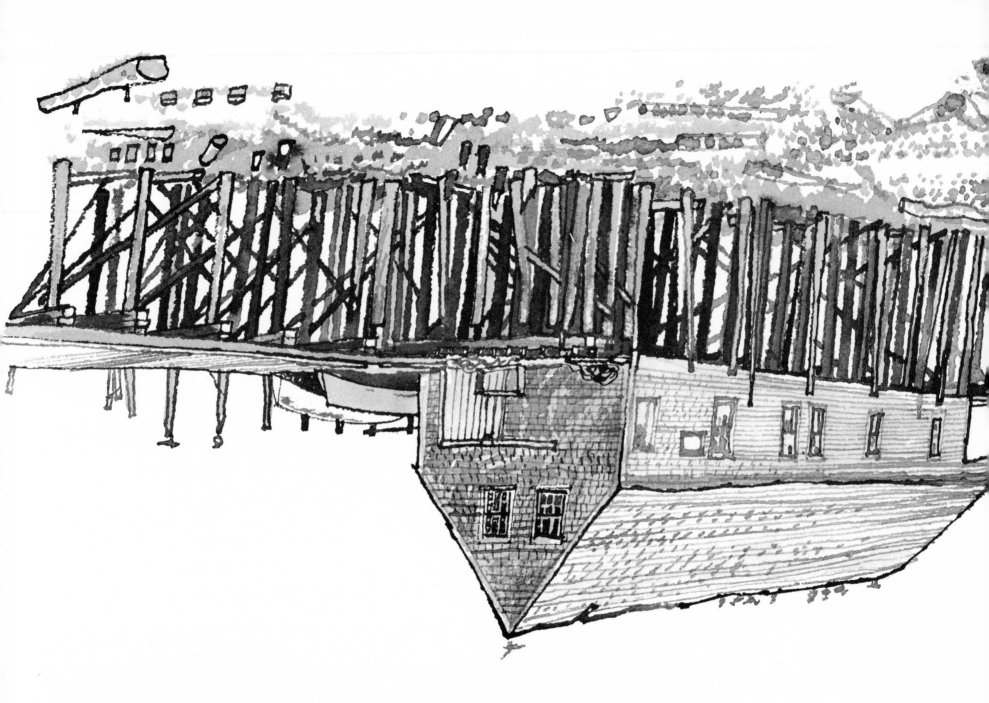

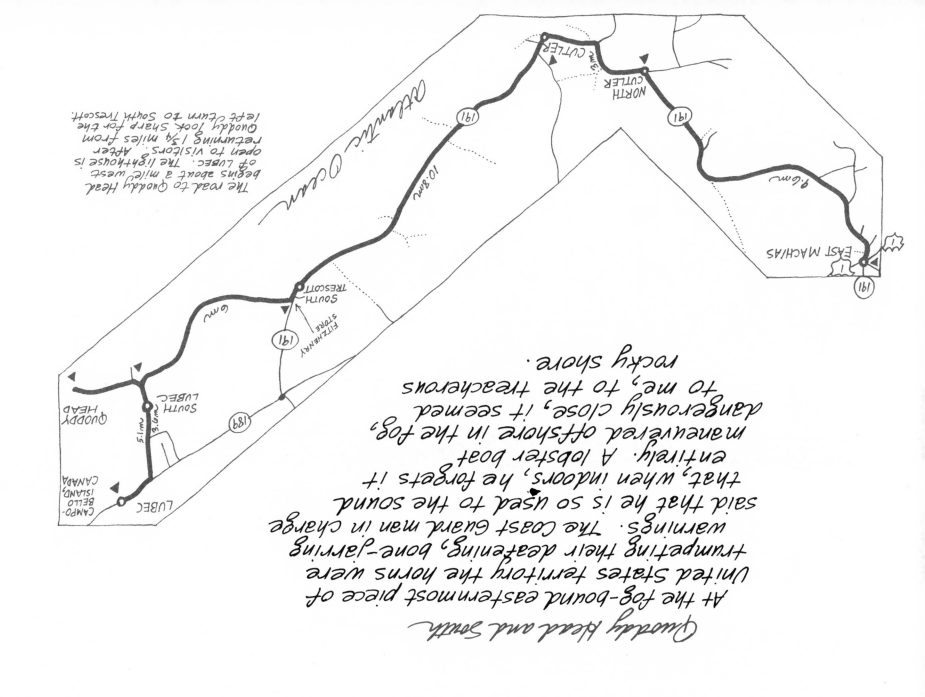

Quoddy Head and South

At the fog-bound easternmost piece of United States territory the horns were trumpeting their deafening, bone-jarring warnings. The Coast Guard man in charge said that he is so used to the sound that, when indoors, he forgets it entirely. A lobster boat maneuvered offshore in the fog, dangerously close, it seemed to me, to the treacherous rocky shore.

The road to Quoddy Head begins about a mile west of LUBEC. The lighthouse is open to visitors. After returning 1¾ miles from Quoddy look sharp for the left turn to South Trescott.

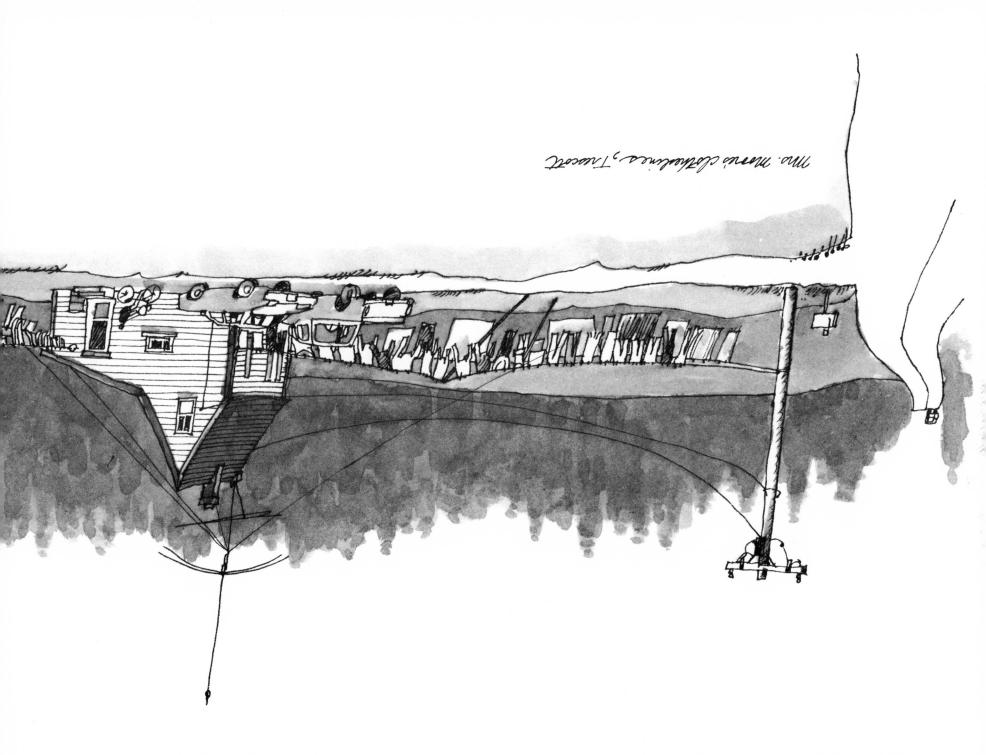

Mrs. Marie Catherine, Tucson

210 Marie Cesar

211

The Road to Cutler

Mrs. Moore has all the room she needs for colorful clotheslines. One line, filled with the wash of her seven children, stretched clear out of my picture into the nearby woods.

From Cutler

Farris wharf has to accommodate a tide of 13 feet. There used to be more wharfs and double the population here in Cutler in the 1930s when fishing favored the smaller fisherman. The boat tied to the wharf is one used to fetch lobsters from lobstermen up and down the coast in the more remote areas and inlets.

The Sawyer House, 1895, Jonesport.

The Road to Jonesport

A Victorian dwelling of multipatterned shingling, the Sawyer house sits prominently by the bay with Beal's Island in the background. A marina is now being built nearby, a place for small pleasure boats and yachts to stop, evidence of the area's change from fishing to tourism as a source of income.

Crossing Moosabec Reach on Bridge Street there are roads to explore on Beal's and Great Wass Island near Jonesport.

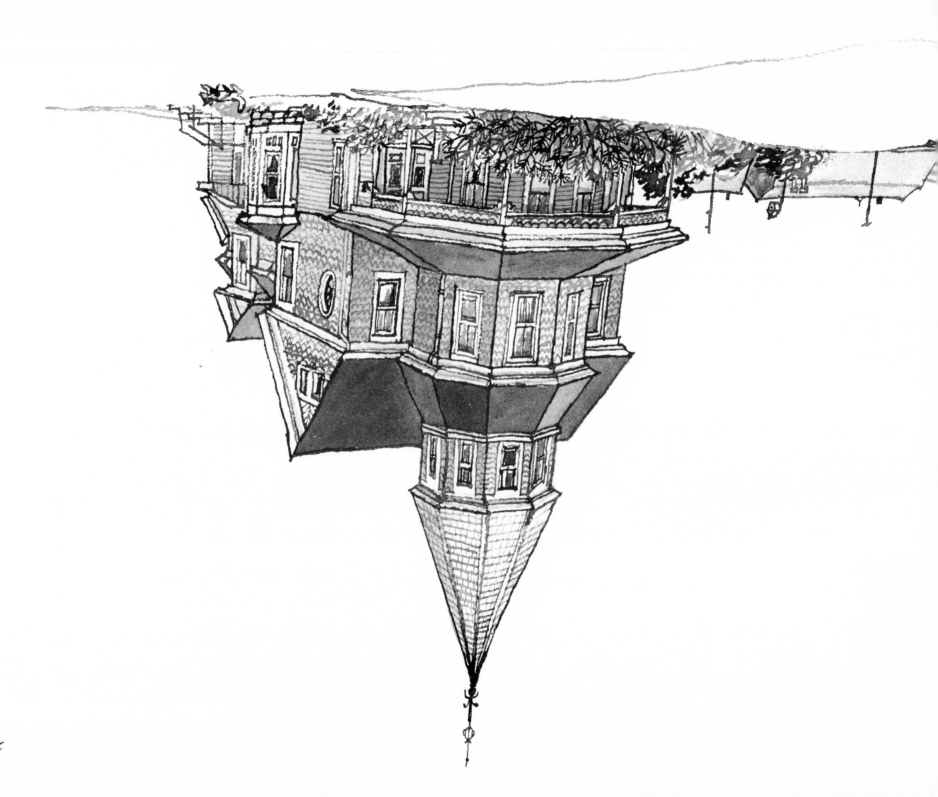

215

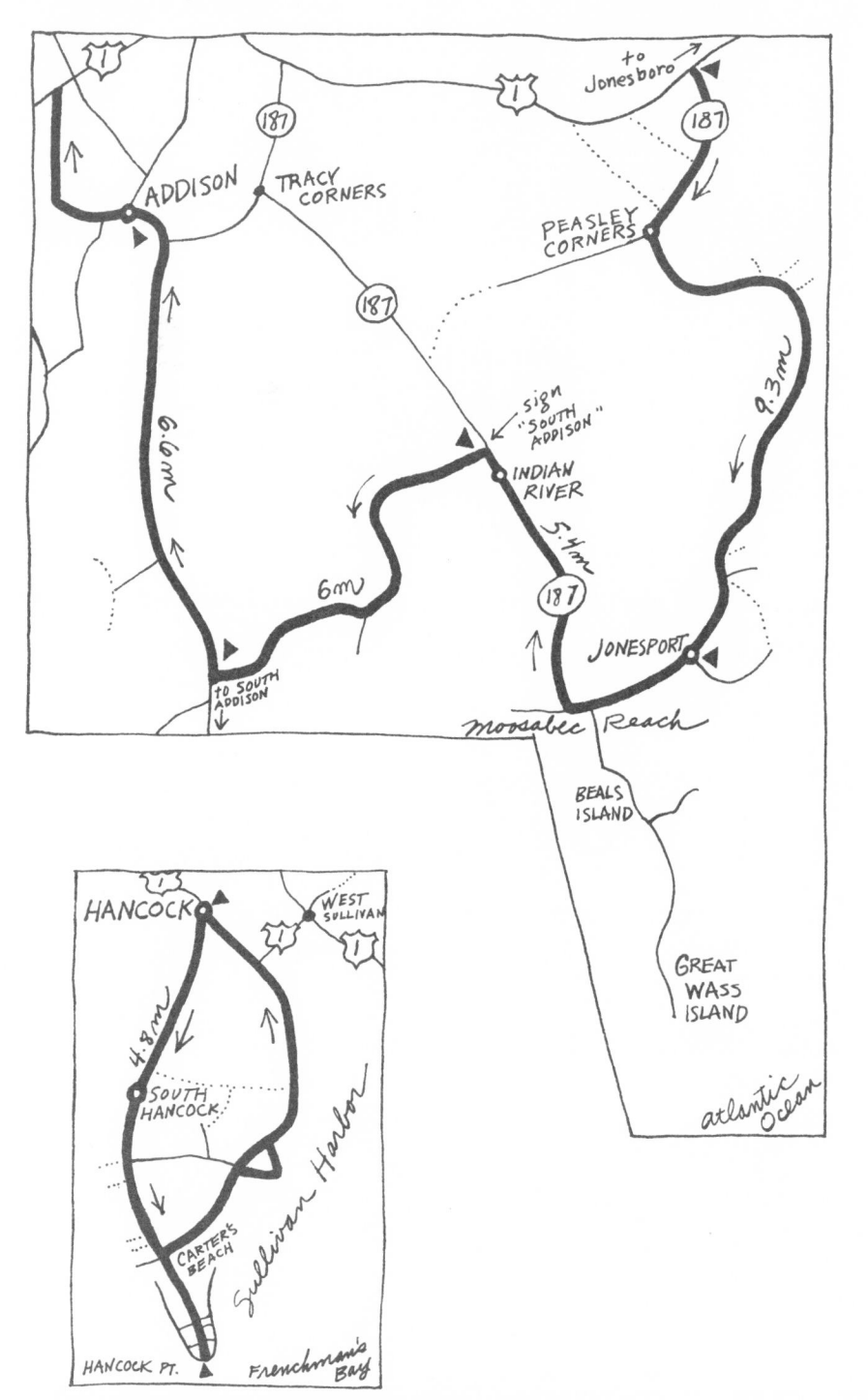

to Jonesboro

1

187

187

ADDISON

TRACY CORNERS

PEASLEY CORNERS

187

6.6m

9.3m

sign "SOUTH ADDISON"

INDIAN RIVER

5.4m

6m

187

to SOUTH ADDISON

JONESPORT

Moosabec Reach

BEALS ISLAND

GREAT WASS ISLAND

atlantic Ocean

HANCOCK

1

WEST SULLIVAN

1

1

4.8m

SOUTH HANCOCK

CARTER'S BEACH

Sullivan Harbor

HANCOCK PT.

Frenchman's Bay

Roads around Hancock

Hancock Point has splendid summer homes nestled among trees and along the shore. The road to Carter's Beach ended on the beach contrary to the map information I had. Views from shore are of many islands and peninsulas.

Cattle Back Hancock Point

Mark and Mel Delando

2/8 Marie Cosat

Road around Schoodic

The road is one way from Winter Harbor around Schoodic Peninsula and emerging at Birch Harbor. Schoodic is part of Acadia National Park and is famous for its crashing surf. My sketch looks toward Mark and Ned, islands that connect at low tide.

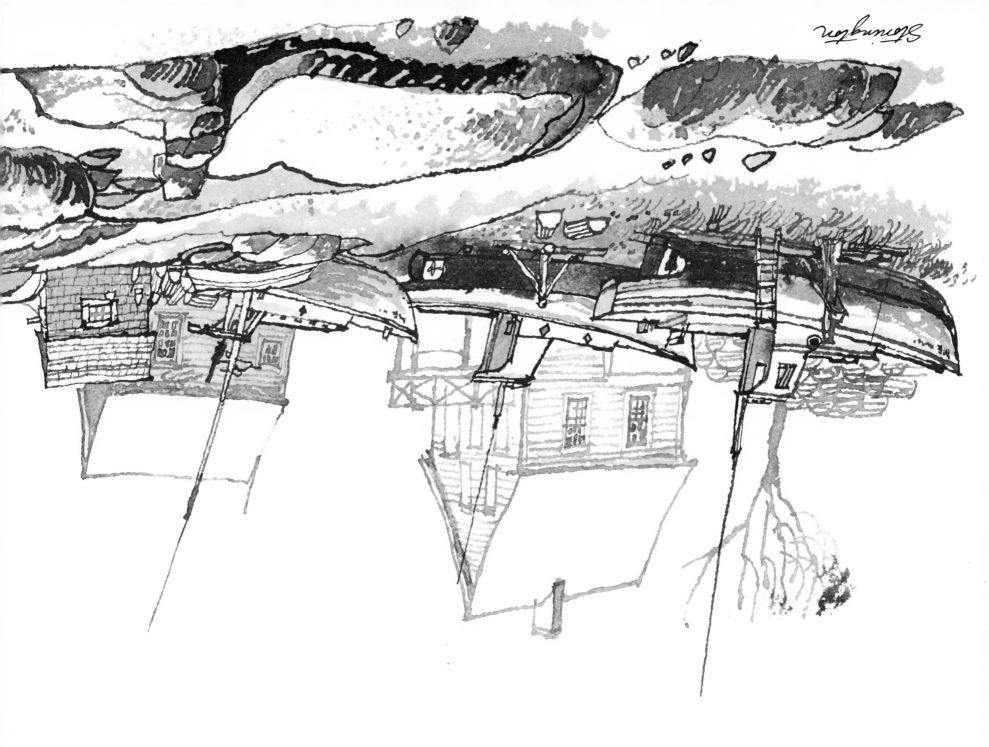

Road to Stonington
The landscape is rolling and beautiful as you drive past tiny harbors and bays. At Stonington I drew a pink granite piece of shore with lobster boats and fishing shacks. I conversed with a young lobster fisherman who gets up at 5 in the morning and home again from the sea at 3 in the afternoon. I asked him if he liked lobstering. "You get used to it," was his reply.

Street sign, Stonington

WESTERN AVE.

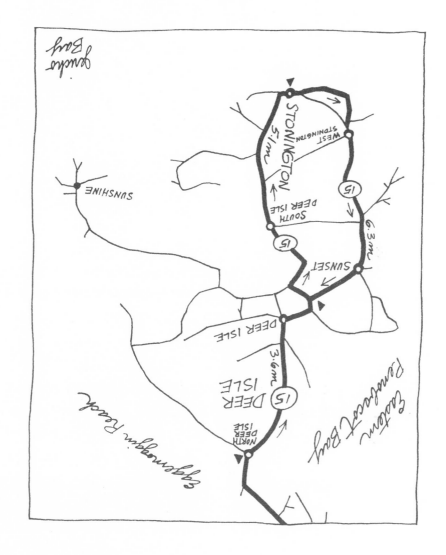

Jericho Bay

STONINGTON

WEST STONINGTON

SUNSHINE

5.1 mi.

15

SOUTH DEER ISLE

6.3 mi.

15

SUNSET

DEER ISLE

3.6 mi.

15

DEER ISLE

NORTH DEER ISLE

Eastern Penobscot Bay

Eggemoggin Reach

222

young deer

Earl Thollander

Epilogue

I wish you to hear the forest and farm sounds, the bird choruses, feel the rocks and the grass, enjoy the spring green, the fall color, and experience the proud heritage of early America through seeing the many historic places in New England. I hope you will make it your plan when you ride the back roads to greet people in friendliness and trust and to take an interest in their way of living.

I urge you to support efforts to protect nature and to preserve structures that express our heritage. This includes steps to improve the automobile, to the point where it no longer is an instrument of pollution. Resist "progress" where it endangers beauty and health and the preservation of historical sites.

The needs of planet earth must now supercede those of mankind, I truly believe.

A Note on This Edition

For this new updated edition of *Back Roads of New England* Mr. Thollander traveled over three thousand miles during September 1981. He found the roads essentially the same as they had been when he originally worked on the book in 1973. The following visual changes were noted. Only one of the Martin houses on page 9 is still standing. On page 67 the railroad crossing sign is gone and on page 111 the entrance of Peter Matteson Tavern has been redone to resemble the original building design. The picket fence is gone; however, another fence is planned. Chiselville's covered bridge, page 113, has lost its picturesque sign. The two buildings on the left on page 157 have been removed. Center Barnstead Christian Church on page 177 is missing some steeple decorations, and the small street in front has been replaced by lawn and several fir trees have been planted. On page 189 the old jail has lost its smokestack. Pike's Wharf, page 207, has been dismantled. Other changes have been noted in the book proper. Extensive editing has improved and made current all maps in the book. Anyone noting discrepancies in the maps or anyone aware of further changes is encouraged to write to the author at House in the Woods, Murray Hill, Calistoga, California 94515.

A Barnes pen, fashioned by myself, was used for most of the drawings in this book. Black, waterproof ink was my medium, along with a bottle of diluted ink for grey tones. An Esterbrook fountain pen with a Speball point and black water-soluble fountain pen ink was used for the other, more delicate sketches. Satté Fair Sudan was employed for washes. The paper used was Fabriano Classico watercolor paper, 140 pound rough for number pen work and Classico 140 pound hot press for fountain pen drawings. All drawings were completed on location.